HACKING GOOGLE
FOR EDUCATION

HACKING GOOGLE FOR EDUCATION

99 Ways to Leverage Google Tools in Classrooms, Schools, and Districts

Brad Currie
Billy Krakower
Scott Rocco

These books are available at special discounts when purchased in quantity for use as premiums, promotions, fundraising, and educational use. For inquiries and details, contact us at www.hacklearning.org.

Published by Times 10
Cleveland, OH
HackLearning.org

Project Management by Rebecca Morris
Cover Design by Tracey Henterly
Interior Design by Steven Plummer
Editing by Ruth Arseneault
Proofreading by Jennifer Jas

Library of Congress Control Number: 2017936321
ISBN: 978-0-9985705-0-1
First Printing: May, 2017

CONTENTS

INTRODUCTION

PICTURE THIS: WHIPPANY, New Jersey, 2001. A class of eighth-grade students sits in a computer lab, typing away, and working alone on word processing documents. Access to the internet is painstakingly slow, and collaboration is intermittent. While working on various projects, students must make sure to continuously click the "save" button so they don't lose their work. There is no way to share the work virtually with other classmates or the teacher. So what is a student to do? Print it out, of course. Feedback on the work is anything but real time. The following week, the teacher hands the marked-up papers back to the students, and they make the necessary corrections. They hit the "save" button and print it out again.

The work can only be completed in class due to the connectivity issues and lack of storage space on the floppy disk. The floppy disk? It's a little plastic thing that people insert into their desktop computer and save their documents. Looking back almost sixteen years, it's amazing people were able to get work done in a timely fashion. But that was the reality for us when we were getting started as educators in New Jersey. Everything took so long to access and save. Collaboration and creation were nowhere near what they are today.

Fast forward to the present, where the internet is accessible to most people and documents can be shared quickly with a tap of the screen or click of the mouse. Paper? What's paper? People can collaborate and make comments on the same document in real time. There is no need to print out paper or save documents on a floppy disk. A school district can become paperless and save money using modern technology. Documents save on their own automatically, and documents can be made accessible in virtual hard drives or in the cloud.

What makes this reality possible? G Suite for Education. With this suite, Google has developed web applications to do tasks similar to those once limited to computer programs. Previously, you needed access to programs that were stored on a computer if you wanted to type a document, create a presentation, or display data. Now you can do these tasks by linking directly to similar applications on the internet. The G Suite applications—Google Docs, Google Slides, Google Sheets, and Google Forms—not only provide users access to information, they present users with the ability to share content from any device in the world that is hooked into the internet. Sharing and collaboration are two of the hallmarks of G Suite for Education.

These innovations have made paperless workflow the norm and have maximized efficiency. The impact of Google's applications on many learning environments, from kindergarten through college, is hard to put into words. Those lucky enough to be a part of a Google environment and its shift in workflow find themselves thriving in ways that once would have been unimaginable.

The intention of this book is to address the needs of multiple audiences. Some of the chapters, or Hacks, are geared for readers working in G Suite districts or looking to make that leap. Other chapters are for everyone: the casual Googler or the experienced district user.

No matter what Google category you're in, it's important to know that we will be using the phrase *G Suite* throughout this book to refer to Google Apps for Education. We will also use Google's term *waffle* to refer to the nine squares, found in the upper right-hand corner of a Google page. These squares allow you to access all Google Apps.

The book contains 33 Hacks. Inside each Hack is a *What You Can Do Tomorrow* section, which offers three ways to apply the Hack, depending on your environment—classroom, school, or district. So, the book contains 99 excellent ways to incorporate G Suite into an educational organization. We have also included a few QR codes: black and white squares that you can use to link to websites or other materials. To take advantage of the QR codes in this book, you will need a QR code reader for your mobile device or tablet. You can download a reader for free in your app store. Once you download the QR code reader, simply scan the QR codes and you'll be whisked off to a bonus resource.

We believe there is a beautiful practicality to this book. With 33 Hacks, featuring 99 tools and strategies, there's value for you. Regardless of your level of expertise, you now have a go-to resource that makes you an expert at everything G Suite.

HACK 1

MAXIMIZE YOUR DIGITAL WORKSPACE WITH THE CHROME BROWSER

THE PROBLEM: INTERNET BROWSERS ARE NOT USER-FRIENDLY

A STUDENT WALKS INTO the classroom, plugs her memory stick into the laptop, and tries unsuccessfully to open up a PowerPoint presentation. Both she and the teacher feel frustrated and unable to understand why the presentation will not work: Neither of them is aware that the laptop is run by Chrome OS. Many of the building's other students encounter similar issues in the coming weeks and months. They learn that sometimes Microsoft products do not play nicely with Google products.

This real-life scenario exemplifies the frustration of educators who are trying to enhance their learning environments. Browsing the internet and navigating certain operating systems can be time-consuming and frustrating. Various browsers and operating systems lack intuition, organizational structure, and synchronization protocols to support school stakeholders. They work in a distinctive environment that has its own challenges and limitations. Usually, the thwarted educator resorts to using a memory stick, which in today's environment seems like the equivalent of writing on a cave wall.

> Forgetting your username or password for education apps will no longer be an issue.

When they encounter difficulty, people will revert back to what they know and feel comfortable with, especially when it comes to technology. Regressing to older habits does not work in an environment where students, teachers, and administrators need to work in a timely, up-to-date fashion.

Brad often works with school districts that use different browsers and operating systems. Inefficient flipping back and forth between browsers muddies workflow in the digital and physical worlds. Staff members frequently experience perplexity when they can't share, open, or edit documents. They are also unable to address technical issues because students or staff are using different programs at the same time. Quite frankly, these minor issues add up to one major—and unnecessary—headache.

THE HACK: USE THE CHROME BROWSER TO SIMPLIFY YOUR ONLINE EXPERIENCE

Install the Chrome OS browser to streamline communication, collaboration, and dissemination of information. Most computers, tablets, and phones will not have Chrome pre-installed unless they're Chromebook or Android devices. Simply put, there is no need for another browser. Since Chrome is your access point to everything Google, it's essential to have it downloaded on your device for immediate access to Google apps and extensions. Scan the QR code in Image 1.1 to access instructions on how to download Chrome on your Windows or Apple devices.

Download the operating system or browser and ensure that it is available on all devices throughout your classrooms, schools, and district. It does not matter if your school is 1:1 with Chromebooks, iPads, or Windows-based laptops. All devices can have the Chrome operating system or browser installed.

Image 1.1

It's important to remember that if your district commits to Chrome, then every student and staff member must have a Google account. That way they can reap the benefits of such programs as Gmail, Drive, Classroom, Docs, Slides, and Sites. Another great feature is the Chrome Store where you add apps and extensions.

As long as you are logged into your Google account you will automatically have access to the apps and extensions that you add. Forgetting your username or password for education apps will no longer be an issue.

Chrome makes quick access to G Suite for Education products very simple: Click the waffle in the upper right-hand side of the screen while in Gmail. Depending on how your waffle is set up you can select YouTube, Calendar, Translate, and many other applications. For the most part, the apps are pre-loaded and can be adjusted by clicking on a specific app and dragging it to a new location. Click on the "More" and "Even More" options to access the entire library of Google apps.

Also make sure to locate the stoplight, the three dots, in the upper right-hand corner of the screen. Once inside Chrome you can access your settings and program the browser to fit your needs. For example, you can select an option to reopen the tab where you left off every time you open the Chrome browser. The suite embeds accessibility features like Search by Voice in the browser, helping those who struggle with typing. You can also select from a variety of languages and change the size of your screen. The best advice we can give you is to jump into the deep end of the Chrome pool and explore all that it has to offer.

Privacy, safety, and restricting accessibility are also features that make Chrome unique and appreciated by users. Once you are in Chrome and logged into your Google account, click on your profile picture in the upper right-hand corner. From here click on the blue "My Account" button to access these various features. For example, in the Personal Privacy and Info section you can conduct a privacy checkup to ensure your YouTube interactions are protected and that photos posted on Google+ cannot be seen by visitors. As you explore, you'll find many more options relating to account settings and sign-in features.

What YOU Can Do Tomorrow

CLASSROOM: Leverage the power of Chrome to create an environment of virtual learning, collaboration, and communication. Commit to the Chrome browser for your virtual learning environment. By taking advantage of all that Chrome has to offer, teachers can create an efficient classroom culture. Chrome facilitates a paperless workflow and a communication system that provides timely feedback. A classroom that once relied on worksheets, stapled packet assessments, and bulky project assignments can now function more efficiently. A teacher can email students through Gmail, comment on work through Google Docs, post assignments on Google Classroom, and give assessments on Google Forms. Students can create, collaborate, and communicate from anywhere in the world.

Reach out to your administration and technology department to inquire about conducting a Chrome pilot. Start out small with one of your classes and expand out as you become more comfortable. During the pilot your class can browse the internet on Chrome, communicate through Gmail, submit assignments on Classroom, and complete assessments on Forms.

SCHOOL: Ensure that all school staff communicate, navigate, create, curate, and collaborate through Chrome. Need to push out or crowdsource an agenda? Create and share a Google Doc. Looking for a way to highlight important information with people in both virtual and physical worlds? Use Google Slides. Want to post important documents and information for faculty meetings? Try Google Classroom. Trying to analyze the effectiveness of a program? Gather feedback with Google Forms.

No other platform has provided administrators the ability to communicate, collect information, and drive change efficiently. It's a mindset and way of life that takes time, but it is well worth the effort. Be patient and see your school culture transform through every click of the mouse or tap of the screen.

DISTRICT: Commit to using the Chrome browser throughout the entire district. District-issued devices will no longer need to have multiple browsers. Being a G Suite for Education district will allow for seamless communication and dissemination of information. More important, it will push stakeholders to create, collaborate, and communicate in unique ways. Chrome makes it possible for a superintendent to conduct a Parent Roundtable Google Hangout. It allows a school district to create an interactive and user-friendly website by way of Google Sites. Chrome allows second graders to learn how to email others using Gmail. It's an all-encompassing initiative that can benefit all stakeholders.

The Chrome operating system, found on all Chromebooks, and the Chrome browser, which can be installed on most devices, help users be more efficient. Chrome turns static environments into interactive communities of learning, teaching, and leading. It is fast, user-friendly, and customizable. Stakeholders from all areas of education can use it in so many ways to enhance their effectiveness and ultimately impact the success of students.

HACK 2

PUT IT IN GOOGLE DRIVE

THE PROBLEM: FILES, FILES EVERYWHERE

NO MATTER WHERE you work—the classroom, principal's office, or the board of education—you have important files and lots of them. Some may be on a desktop; some may be on your personal laptop; others might be sitting on your Smartphone. When you need that one file most, it may be impossible to access.

Since Google is cloud-based, all files are automatically saved to your Google account in your Google Drive. Still, even powerful cloud-based filing systems need to be organized. Depending on how active your Drive is, it can become overwhelmed with the various Docs, Sheets, Forms, and Folders you create and those that are shared with you. So it is vital to your job and sanity to get organized from the start and understand the ways to set up your Drive and how to share specific files and folders.

> It's no longer necessary to tediously download each file one at a time and then drag it into the folder you want. Google Drive makes it easier.

THE HACK: SET UP AND ORGANIZE YOUR DRIVE FOLDERS EFFECTIVELY FROM THE BEGINNING

An organized Drive and an understanding of its features will make you a more efficient educator in the classroom, school, and district. Scott has spent a great deal of time organizing his Drive into folders that allow him easy access to the files he needs the most. His organization has allowed him to access information in his various roles as a superintendent, adjunct professor, keynote speaker, and coach for his son's sports teams.

Google Drive is easy to access once you sign in to your Gmail account. Go up to the waffle and then click on "Drive". A new tab will open up with all of your files in it. Many different features in Drive allow you to create files and folders, share files and folders, preview files, move files and folders, view details, organize folders, and sync files so you can work offline. The features in Google Drive provide educators with many options to make it more than a place to store files. It's a place to efficiently and effectively organize everything that can be stored in a folder.

What
YOU
Can Do Tomorrow

CLASSROOM: Create a shared classroom folder in Drive.
A powerful feature of Google is the ability to share with students and then collaborate on a shared file. Every one of Google's apps can be shared easily. From your waffle open Drive and select "New folder." A new window called "New folder" will open. Name the folder, perhaps using the name of the assignment or the class and click the "Create" button. Now go to the folder and right click on it with your mouse. You'll be offered a series of choices with this folder; click the "Share" feature. Again, the new window will give you choices. You can choose to set the folder to view or edit. "View only" allows students to see the folder. "Edit" allows students to make changes.

It's important to note that the Share setting for the folder determines the setting for all files in that folder. So the final choice in this section is to shut the folder sharing off and specifically designate who has access. To share it with specific students, identify them by typing their email addresses in the area below the "People" section. Then use the drop-down menu next to the pencil on the right side to designate what type of access people have to the folder and its contents. Click "Done" and the folder is shared.

Bonus: You can also change the color of the folder in your Drive by right clicking the folder and selecting the "Change color" option in the drop-down menu. If you like to color code things as Scott does, you will love this feature.

SCHOOL: Create a shared professional development Doc in Drive for participants to take notes collaboratively. Google Docs provides the ability to collaborate during professional learning using a shared Doc in Drive. You can set up a template or just allow people to create a shared Doc where they can provide information and content from the professional development throughout the day. Setting up a Doc starts with logging into your Google account and then opening Drive and clicking "New" on the top left. Once there, select "Google Docs." If you want a clean form with no template, then set up the Doc that just opened by putting a title in the area labeled "Untitled document" on the top left.

Bonus: Type the title on the top of your Doc and then click your cursor in the "Untitled document" section on the top left. Voila: Your title is there, and you've saved a step.

If you want a template or just want to see your choices, click the blue box on the top left, which is called "Docs home." This maneuver will bring up a template gallery that you can use to customize your Doc. Once you have chosen a type of Doc, you are ready to share by clicking on the "Share" button on the top left of your computer screen. A new window called "Share with others" will pop up. Depending on the purposes of your collaboration, you'll need to decide whether you want to give people the ability to edit documents or if they just need to view them. Since we are talking about collaboration, click the "Anyone with the link can view" option on the top. To share this Doc with collaborators, copy the link and paste it into an email, or you can enter email addresses in the section labeled "People" at the bottom of the form. Then select the "Can edit" option to the right on the drop-down menu located next to the pencil. Click "Done" and you have a collaborative Doc for everyone at your professional day.

Check out Hack 5 for more information on collaborating and commenting in Docs.

DISTRICT: Download all files attached to an email to a specific Drive folder. It seems like at least once a week district administrators get an email that has multiple files attached to it. It's no longer necessary to tediously download each file one at a time and then drag it into the folder you want. Google Drive makes it easier.

Open the email and scroll to the bottom where the files are listed. You should see the Drive symbol. Scroll over it with your cursor and it should say, "Save all to Drive." Click "Save all to Drive" and then an option will pop up that says "Organize." Press it. Your Drive folders will pop up in the window, and you can select the folder where you want these files to be stored. Or you can hit the "+" symbol on the bottom of a file. This allows you to put it in a new folder that doesn't exist yet and name that folder.

To boost your ability to organize even more, you can save these files in folders that are inside of other folders. For example, a folder for a specific school in your district could contain folders for each department in the school. The download will allow you to select the specific department or even a folder inside that folder. Who wouldn't be excited about this feature?

Drive is more than a place for your files to go. It can be a color-coded, organized space that provides access to anyone with whom you choose to share. Most important, it will make managing all your incoming files so easy that you'll never be stressed looking for something because you know it's there.

HACK 3

MAKE GMAIL WORK FOR YOU

THE PROBLEM: EMAIL CAN BE A BURDEN THAT CONSUMES PRECIOUS TIME

Y EARS AGO RECEIVING an email was exciting, so you'd enjoy taking time to craft a reply. Today, our inboxes are crammed full of emails. Many of us maintain multiple email addresses, which complicates the already complex daily ritual of deciding which unread messages are important and need to be addressed immediately, which can wait, and which can go directly to the trash. For many educators, opening email can be a burden because the task of determining what needs to be addressed and what doesn't eats into time needed to prepare for another school day.

> **Opening your inbox in Gmail doesn't have to be an unmanageable and overwhelming experience.**

Scott struggled with the email burden because he maintained an email account for his work as a superintendent of schools, another for his position as an adjunct professor, and a third for his personal life. Seeing 900 unread messages on his phone app became an overwhelming burden. Add to this pressure the tweets from colleagues and friends like Rich Kiker, who boast about their ability to get their inbox to zero. Scott thought there had to be a better way to get organized, respond to the important emails, and delete those that clog up the inbox. So he started harnessing the power of Gmail and made it work for him.

THE HACK: USE GMAIL FEATURES
TO ORGANIZE EMAILS

Gmail is more than an email service. Its amazing features will organize your email and your time. It will quickly control your inbox and end your struggle with organizing and filtering emails. Get familiar with the search box at the top of your Gmail page. This versatile tool has multiple functions to get you organized quickly and to filter emails.

Clicking the downward triangle to the left of the blue search button opens up a world of options in your Gmail. The first of these searches your email. By clicking on this button you search your email by specific default folder or by the folders you establish—its default is "All Mail." You can also search only unread emails or those you have already reviewed. This search option will prove useful when you are looking to clean out your email inbox immediately. You can also search for emails that have attachments, are a specific size, or are from a specific date range. Once you get comfortable with those Gmail features, you can take filtering further by creating custom filters for your emails so Gmail works for you.

What
YOU
Can Do Tomorrow

CLASSROOM: Create folders for each of your classes.
One of the main reasons we lose control of our many inboxes is that we don't take advantage of email features that organize incoming messages. Any classroom teacher would benefit from developing folders that store emails after you answer them. You can organize these folders by subject (for example, *Science Class*), or by period (for example, *Period 4 World History*). We also suggest you add the school year or

some way of identifying sections: *Pd 4 WH 2017-18* would represent period 4 World History in the 2017-18 school year.

Creating a folder is simple: Click on the box to the left of an email, which will give you access to a row of features, including a folder. Select the folder feature, click "Create new," and name the folder. You will see the folder icon in Image 3.1. If you want to take your organization a step further, use the "Nest label under" feature to put the folder inside another folder. From this point on you can simply drag messages into the folder or click the box to the left of the email and then identify which folder you want to send your message to on the folders icon.

Image 3.1 Google and the Google logo are registered trademarks of Google Inc., used with permission.

Creating folders and putting emails in those folders will help you organize and declutter your inbox so you can find emails faster. It will also help you get your inbox to the often unattainable zero unread messages goal.

SCHOOL: Create labels for grade-level staff, departments, and/or committees. Every school organization consists of many different groups: grade-level groups, subject-specific departments, various committees, parent organizations, and outside affiliations. One of the best ways to keep track of the information regarding these different groups is to create labels for your emails.

The process of creating a label is identical to creating a folder. Labels identify types of emails, such as emails from staff members, whereas folders serve as a place to hold those messages. To create a label, click on the box to the left of the email you want to label. Then, find the label tab to the right of the folder tab at the top of your screen. Clicking on it will allow you to create a new label and manage existing labels. You will see the label icon in Image 3.1.

Scott found two exciting things about using labels. First, you can put more than one label on an email. Second, once you establish a label for a specific sender, that label is automatically put on the email when it is sent to your inbox. This makes putting it in a folder that much easier.

You need to develop a system for your labels. Just as with your folder names, you need to create a structure. Although it's up to you, it's a good idea to include the group or organization. We suggest not including a year since labels are for specific senders and may span more than a year. For example, you may be on a professional development committee that is not limited to one school year.

DISTRICT: Create a filter for emails coming from a specific person or organization. If you work at the district level, many different people and organizations email you. If you're on a number of mailing lists, emails from organizations or businesses can really clutter your inbox. You can manage all types of emails by creating filters for them and letting Gmail work for you as they come into your inbox.

Creating a filter is as easy as creating a folder or a label. First, click on the upside-down triangle in the Gmail search box. Then, input criteria for the search you want to do. It can be a specific email address sending you the message, a specific subject that many people are responding to, or any of the other choices the search box gives you as filtering criteria. Once you have the criteria in the search area, you will notice at the bottom of the drop-down menu there is a feature called "Create filter with this search." It will turn blue once you enter criteria. Click on it. Look at Image 3.2 to see all the ways you can filter this type of email.

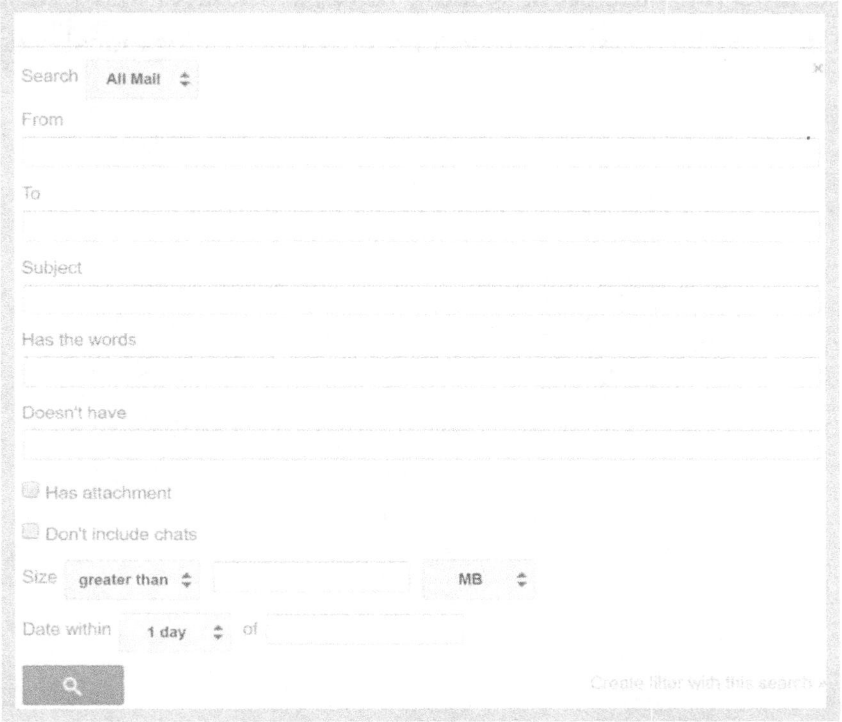

Image 3.2 Google and the Google logo are registered trademarks of Google Inc., used with permission.

Using filter criteria, you can weed out emails from particular senders by clicking on "Delete it." If you want to attach a label, click on "Apply the label" and then identify the label from the drop-down menu. You can highlight essential messages with the "Always mark it as important" option. Don't be limited to just one filter. You can put multiple filters on emails.

Opening your inbox in Gmail doesn't have to be an unmanageable and overwhelming experience. By organizing it with specific folders, using labels, and creating email filters, you will get control of those emails. You'll also get back the time you once spent reading through messages and figuring out what to do with them. Use that time for more exciting educational endeavors.

HACK 4

SYNC ALL EVENTS WITH CALENDAR

THE PROBLEM: I NEED TO FIND ALL
DISTRICT EVENTS AT ONCE

S CHOOL DISTRICTS ARE known for having complex, confusing schedules, and events that all seem to be going on at once. The range of special events, board of education meetings, staff meetings, and social gatherings can become overwhelming and hard to keep track of. A passing glance of Brad's schedule, for instance, showed a meeting regarding the New Jersey Assistant Principal of the Year award reception along with a board of education meeting. Billy's had an IEP meeting nearly overlapping with a parent meeting. Managing hectic schedules has become a struggle for many educators in many school districts.

Making sure all stakeholders have the correct dates, times, and locations can also be a challenge. When so many different events are occurring, communication and event details can often be missed. With Google Calendar as part of G Suite, scheduling has become more efficient.

> **With Google's calendar function, parents, students, or staff members can choose which calendar they want to subscribe to, or they can subscribe to multiple calendars at once and get alerts to their Gmail accounts.**

THE HACK: SHARE IMPORTANT DATES AND EVENTS WITH GOOGLE CALENDAR

Google Calendar allows districts, buildings, and classrooms to share important dates and events with a few clicks of the mouse. Several different calendars can be created so that any departmental needs can be met. Each group can share events on a public calendar, or a calendar can apply to a specific group of people. Not only can staff members add to the calendar, but parent groups can add their events to the calendar as well. Parents, students, or staff members can choose which calendar they want to subscribe to or they can subscribe to multiple calendars at once and get alerts to their Gmail accounts. There's no need to miss another event or have another occasion flop because people were unaware of it.

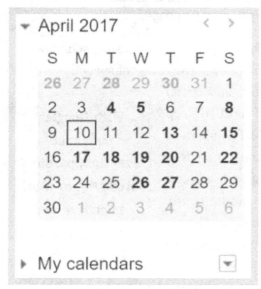

Image 4.1 Google and the Google logo are registered trademarks of Google Inc., used with permission.

Here are the simple steps to creating a shared space calendar. From the waffle, open your Google Calendar. You will see on the left side the category "My calendars" and a downward arrow. Image 4.1 will show you "My calendars." Click the arrow. Click "Create new calendar." You can now name the calendar and add a description in the new screen that pops up. Add the specific location this calendar references.

Now you select your sharing options. By selecting "Make this calendar public," the calendar is searchable and people will be able to view the details. For scheduling space in a school or district, we recommend using the "Share with specific people" option below the "Make this calendar public" section. Insert the email addresses of everyone you want to share this calendar with and then choose their permission settings on the right. To allow those people to schedule times, you will want to select "Make changes to events" in the permissions settings.

What
YOU
Can Do Tomorrow

CLASSROOM: Set up a Classroom Calendar. When you create a class in Google Classroom, you automatically create a Google Calendar. A shared classroom calendar allows teachers to communicate homework, tests, and other important information. You'll no longer need to worry about students forgetting to write down their homework or bring home their assignment planners. Students and parents will be able to view all of the assignments from any device that supports G Suite.

There are several ways to share out a Google Calendar in addition to subscribing. One option is to embed your classroom calendar on a webpage. Under "Calendar details" in Settings locate "Embed this calendar," then copy and paste the code on the specific webpage where you want the calendar to be displayed. Another option is to use and display the calendar that goes along with the classroom you created in Google Classroom. This way any assignments or announcements that you post will automatically show on the calendar.

SCHOOL: Streamline building communication with the invite feature. Principals can use Calendar's invite feature to inform teachers of important committee meetings and keep track of attendees. The invite feature allows you to invite participants through their email addresses. If the user you are inviting has a Google account, the invite will automatically appear on his or her calendar. This is great, not just for meetings with teachers, but also for meetings with parents. Brad will often invite colleagues to important meetings using the invite feature when he sets up the event in Calendar. Those staff members who are invited can select yes, maybe, or no through the alert that appears in their email or pops up on the actual calendar. Brad is able to then keep a running tab on who has replied and who is able to attend.

DISTRICT: Provide a district-wide calendar to share a specific space.

Limited physical space in schools and districts makes scheduling difficult. The old way was to put a calendar on the wall where people would sign up for times. Sometimes a secretary would book the room and times. These inefficient ways of sharing space limited access to the people who could find time to walk down to the space and write on the calendar or place a call. Sharing the calendar for a conference room or professional development space easily and efficiently syncs events and activities. It also allows people in your district the opportunity to take control of their scheduling. Start small and try a shared calendar for signing up to use the conference room in the board of education office. Make sure to select the "Share only free/busy information" so others know when the space is available.

School districts are busy places with overwhelming, often confusing schedules, and many events that all seem to be going on at once. Making sure everyone has the correct dates and places to be on their calendars and the ability to schedule space is vital to the operation of the district. Calendar takes the struggle out of the process and makes everyone more efficient.

HACK 5

COLLABORATE AND COMMENT IN DOCS

THE PROBLEM: COLLABORATION AND FEEDBACK RARELY HAPPEN IN REAL TIME

GOOGLE DOCS, A collaborative, real-time word processing program, gives users an opportunity to create, share, and provide feedback with ease. It's the ultimate tool for stakeholders to post initial content and see progress toward the finished product through various stages. Educators may overlook the true potential of the comment feature in Google Docs to provide feedback in a timely fashion. Many factors contribute to their oversight, including a lack of support and training. We could achieve numerous goals and save many hours through real-time collaboration.

Taking two weeks to hand back grades on paper does not help anyone. Writing up a committee report; emailing it to colleagues; and waiting days, sometimes weeks or months, for input can be frustrating. Fortunately, we now can slash those time gaps with Google Docs. Docs can be used to enhance efficiency, communication, and impact the success of students in the classroom, school, or district setting. From sharing a document with another person to collaborating on a document with someone in real time, Google Docs makes many things possible.

> No longer will people be unsure of their progress or what needs to be done.

THE HACK: USE THE COMMENT FEATURE TO OPEN UP A DIALOGUE WITH STUDENTS

One of the single most important things that Google Docs enables educators to do is provide real-time feedback. The comment feature in Google Docs can assist teachers in providing timely feedback on an assignment before, during, or after school. It can help district-level personnel update an important document in a timely and flexible way. A Google Docs user can create and edit a document on any device in the world with or without internet access. Go into the Drive settings and check the offline feature; this way you can work on a document offline and it will sync up when you go online.

Here are a few tips to help you navigate through the various efficiency features of Google Docs:

- In order to share the Google Doc with other collaborators, click on the "Share" button in the upper right-hand corner of the document. From there, the names or email addresses of the staff members or students who you want to share the document with must be entered into the box. Then a certain type of editing right needs to be chosen: "Can edit," "Can comment," or "Can view."

- Enable the comment feature by clicking on the "Comment" button in the upper right-hand corner of the page. Then, highlight the text you want to comment on within the Doc. See Image 5.1 for what the button looks like.

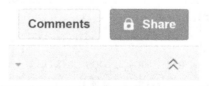

Image 5.1 Google and the Google logo are registered trademarks of Google Inc., used with permission.

- While collaborating on the same Doc, you will notice that each collaborator has a different color to delineate who is working on what part of the document.

- You can chat with fellow collaborators by clicking on the chat box in the lower right-hand corner of the screen.

What YOU Can Do Tomorrow

CLASSROOM: **Provide relevant and timely feedback on student work.** Say for example your language arts students are assigned to draft a piece of writing. It's important that students share their Docs with you. That way you will have access to the document and can make timely comments as the students are working on their drafts. Highlight the text you want to comment on and then click on the "Add a comment" icon that pops up on the side of the document.

Make sure to keep yourself sane and organized by turning off email notifications and ensure that workflow is pushed through Google Classroom or a shared Drive folder. You can adjust notifications by clicking the gray "Comments" button in the upper right-hand corner of the screen. Then, click on "Notifications" and select from the options.

On their end, students see the comments on the side of their documents and can implement the corrections to improve their writing and know right away how they are progressing.

SCHOOL: **Tell your school's story with digital tools.** Use Google Docs to curate and disseminate a monthly report highlighting student and staff achievements. In the weeks leading up to the monthly report's publication, a school administrator can open up editing rights to the Google Doc for staff members so they can add information about the great things going on in their classrooms or extracurricular activities.

In this case the "Can edit" option should be chosen and the "Send" button clicked. From this point forward staff members have the ability to edit the document as they see fit. Once all of the edits and additions have been made to the monthly report, it can be shared out and embedded on various applications in the virtual world, including websites, blogs, tweets, and Facebook feeds, to name a few. To embed a Google Doc on your website, click on the "File" tab at the top of the screen, click on "Publish to the web," and copy and paste the embed code to your website or blog.

DISTRICT: Encourage a paperless workflow for your entire organization. Recently, Brad was tasked with updating and digitizing his district's crisis management plan. Brad took the old 150-page document out of the binder, scanned the documents on the copy machine, emailed the scanned copies as a PDF to his account, and transferred them to Google Docs. From there, Brad disseminated the Google Doc to key stakeholders in the district so they could comment on and edit the parts they were responsible for.

At the district level Google Docs can be used in many ways to maintain a paperless workflow and promote collaboration. Once the revision process is over, the document will be housed in a private shared Drive for all staff to access. This will ensure everyone is abreast of the plan and can act appropriately during a crisis. In the unfortunate event that a crisis occurs, staff will be able to access the plan from any device in the world.

Google Docs provides users with an opportunity to collaborate and offer insight in an efficient way. Its handy real-time aspect always keeps people on track. No longer will people be unsure of their progress or what needs to be done. In fact, you can click on "File" and "See revision history" to go back, look at changes, and see how far you've come. Start today and commit to a paperless workflow culture that streamlines communication and moves everyone forward on a positive path.

HACK 6

EXTEND THE CAPABILITY OF DOCS

THE PROBLEM: DOING THINGS ON
PAPER SLOWS EFFICIENCY

BRAD CAN VIVIDLY remember creating and using paper rubrics to assess student projects in his social studies classes. Although the rubrics served an important purpose, they were sometimes misplaced by students while they were working on their assignments. The elements of the rubric were sometimes difficult to match up with the specific parts of the students' assignments, meaning that elements might have been too general. Often students had a hard time reading the feedback. Many of them responded better to a voice than to written feedback. Brad always thought that there must be a better way.

Let's not forget about you, and how at one time or another you've probably needed to jazz up a document you created in a word processing program so students or staff could gain a deeper understanding of a topic. You've probably wanted a way to enhance communication on the content of a word processing document so you could get clearer feedback. Formalizing word processing documents was never easy. Maybe you needed a signature or maybe you needed someone to fill in information. That used to involve printing the document out, faxing it, and then waiting for a return fax. The process was less than ideal and took what seemed like an eternity. Fortunately,

> **Google Doc Add-ons bring an unparalleled functionality to Google Docs.**

Google Docs features now enhance the user experience. Over the past several years, technology has given people an opportunity to embed and edit documents in multiple ways.

THE HACK: USE ADD-ONS TO GET THE MOST OUT OF DOCS

Take advantage of a little-known feature of Google Docs called Add-ons. These enhancements are different from an app or extension in that they specifically address a user's need within Google Docs. The first thing you want to do is open up a Google Doc and locate the "Add-ons" tab at the top of the screen. When you click on that tab, you will notice a box split in two parts. The first part of the box contains Add-ons that you've already chosen. The second part of the box allows you to find new Add-ons and manage previously selected Add-ons. Take a look at Image 6.1 for the options listed in Add-ons.

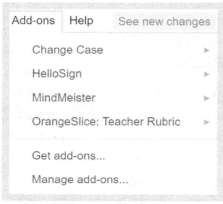

Image 6.1 Google and the Google logo are registered trademarks of Google Inc., used with permission.

At this point click on "Get add-ons" and browse the various kinds that are available. You'll see everything from an Add-on for creating citations to one for finding synonyms. When you find an Add-on that might be useful, simply click the blue button that says "Free." You will now notice that the Add-on is viewable in the options menu. To activate an Add-on, click on it and follow the instructions.

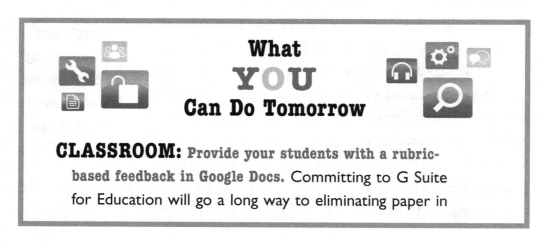

What YOU Can Do Tomorrow

CLASSROOM: Provide your students with a rubric-based feedback in Google Docs. Committing to G Suite for Education will go a long way to eliminating paper in your classroom. Try the Add-on OrangeSlice to help you grade essays on Google Docs. Once you add and activate OrangeSlice, a menu appears on the right-hand side of the page that will assist with customizing your rubric. The components of the rubric vary and include performance-level progressions, performance levels, and categories. Select your options for the rubric, click the "Create Rubric" button at bottom, and set to work grading. Students can submit a Google Doc through Google Classroom, hand you a hard copy of a paper, or send it via email.

Image 6.2 Google and the Google logo are registered trademarks of Google Inc., used with permission.

The rubric will now be visible at the top of the document and you can edit content as needed.

Added bonus: Download OrangeSlice: Student Rubric so students can assess each other with their very own rubrics.

SCHOOL: Turn a Google Doc's bullet points into a visually appealing mind map with the MindMeister Add-on. Notes you take during a faculty meeting, staff inservice, PLC, subject-area meeting, or grade-level meeting are usually not very visually appealing. Enter the MindMeister Google Doc Add-on: It will take your bulleted list items and transform them into a beautiful mind map. Open up a Google Doc that contains bulleted list items, download the MindMeister Add-on, highlight the content that you want displayed, activate the MindMeister Add-on, and then watch it organize your bullet points into a mind map. The generated image and your bulleted content get saved in the Google Doc.

DISTRICT: Formalize a Google Doc with a digital signature using the HelloSign Add-on. Let's face it, central office administrators have to sign off on a lot of documents every day. Many of these documents require a digital signature. The HelloSign Google Doc Add-on makes digital signatures a snap. To get things started make sure to scan Image 6.3 with your QR code reader and sign up for an account. The free version gives you the opportunity to sign three free documents per month. The paid version allows for unlimited signatures, and costs anywhere from $13 to $60 per month depending on what plan is selected.

Once you have signed up for the Add-on, open up the Google Doc. Activate the HelloSign Add-on by adding it to  the menu that appears on the right-hand side of the page and selecting "Sign Document." A menu will then appear on the left-hand side of the page. Click the blue tab that says "Draw New Signature." At

Image 6.3

this point you sign your name and click inside of the box that contains your digital signature. You can then select the "Email as PDF" option to email the signed PDF document to a recipient. This feature allows you to complete the whole process in Docs without having to open additional programs like Adobe.

Google Doc Add-ons bring unparalleled functionality to Google Docs. The enhancements provide educators with more efficient ways to deal with time-consuming administrative items. Add-ons can also make your Google Doc look more appealing and provide embedded functionality for grading. Start today by trying out just one of the Add-ons mentioned in this chapter. Better yet, find one that was not mentioned in this chapter and see if it works for you.

LIFT DATA TO NEW HEIGHTS WITH SHEETS

THE PROBLEM: I NEED A PLACE TO PUT DATA

DEALING WITH THE data generated by assessments is an unavoidable—and time-consuming—part of teaching. Similarly, administrators collect extensive data: student assessments, teacher observations, parent information, and district goals. All of this data can overwhelm even the most efficient of educators, and furthermore, it's hard to find effective ways to share findings with students, parents, and other educators. Google Sheets makes organizing and collecting data simple.

Sheets interacts with another G Suite program called Google Forms, which we will talk about in Hack 9. Together, these two programs will put an end to your data headaches.

THE HACK: MAKE DATA EASY AGAIN WITH SHEETS

To begin work in Sheets, sign in to your Google account, and access Drive through the waffle. Go to the "New" button and select "Google Sheets" to start work in a blank sheet. Sheets is similar to Microsoft Excel in that they both have rows and columns that are lettered and numbered. Sheets has many functions including the ability to calculate formulas that you input into selected

> Sheets also allows the user to create a graph of relevant data.

rows and columns. Sheets includes numerous different formulas to generate various types of useful information. Scan the QR code in Image 7.1 to view a list of all the formulas supported in Sheets.

Do not get scared if you have never used formulas before. They are easy and user-friendly. All you have to do is put the = sign, followed by the formula you want to use. For instance, if you want to ditch the paper gradebook and go dig-

ital, Sheets formulas make it simple. First, create a student roster for your class. Then input student grades into columns and use one of the formulas in Sheets to calculate the average. You would input =AVERAGE( ). The column and row numbers you want to compute go inside the ( ).

Image 7.1

Sheets also allows the user to create a graph of relevant data. Furthermore, tabs at the bottom of Sheets allow a user to add multiple sheets to one document. This is great for a school or district that needs to collect the same data from multiple grades or areas: All the necessary data stays in one document.

What YOU Can Do Tomorrow

CLASSROOM: Students can create a graph and break down data. If you are conducting a science experiment such as the heating of materials, students can record their information into Sheets and then create a graph to visually represent the information. Another example would be for students to test catapults they build in STEM class and record the distances on Google Sheets. Then students can create graphs and share out to classmates for analysis through Google Classroom.

SCHOOL: In New Jersey, Brad uses Sheets to organize Intervention and Referral Services data. Sheets helps streamline the way in which teachers are able to view data for students who are in need of extra support. Rather than having multiple sources of information, use Sheets to input the information and create a tab for each student. You can apply this organizational strategy for any data that is being collected. To make things even easier, create a Form to collect the information and review the data in Sheets.

DISTRICT: Districts can track student progress and performance. Create a privately shared Google Sheet so district staff can find and use shared data to inform instruction. For example, maintain a district-wide Google Sheet that categorizes standardized test scores over several years to identify strengths and weaknesses in student performance. Teachers from various schools will be able to stay current with student progress. It would also be beneficial to add other data points such as class grades and benchmark assessments.

When educators use Google Sheets effectively, they can drive change and store important information in one shared location. Having access to important student data can keep all stakeholders, including parents and students, informed at annual meetings and conferences. What's more, Google Sheets provides users an opportunity to create visually appealing graphs and charts with a few clicks of the mouse. Start small in one particular school by giving Google Sheets a try at a team meeting where you are tasked with breaking down data. Over time it will become a part of the district culture.

BOOST YOUR SPREADSHEET WITH SHEETS ADD-ONS

THE PROBLEM: THERE ARE UNTAPPED RESOURCES IN SHEETS

BRAD CAN DISTINCTLY remember a time as a young administrator when he was given a spreadsheet with an enormous amount of testing data. He needed to dissect the data within a few days and present his findings at an upcoming faculty meeting. It was overwhelming to say the least. He always thought there was a better way, but technology had not caught up to spreadsheet functionality.

Luckily technology is catching up, and there are many ways to simplify and share data.

THE HACK: USE GOOGLE SHEETS ADD-ONS TO SIMPLIFY DATA

Take advantage of Google Sheets Add-ons to get the most out of your spreadsheet. Open up a Google Sheet and locate the "Add-ons" tab at the top of the screen just as in Doc Add-ons. From here you can click the tab and see the Add-ons that you have added in the past, get Add-ons, and manage Add-ons. Browse through "Get Add-ons" and see what would serve your spreadsheet needs the most efficiently. You can find everything from lab schedulers to cell splitters. Once you've added your choices, you can manage them by clicking on "Manage Add-ons."

What
YOU
Can Do Tomorrow

CLASSROOM: Create virtual flashcards to study for an upcoming quiz or test with the Flippity Add-on. Open up a Google Sheet and download the Flippity Add-on. You will see that Flippity shows up as an option under the "Add-ons" tab. Image 8.1 shows what the Add-on looks like. It will provide you with several templates to choose from, the first of which is flashcards. Select the flashcards option and notice data has been added to your spreadsheet. The next step will be to add your own information to the spreadsheet. For example, in a social studies class you might be studying states and capitals. So you would type in the states in one column and the corresponding capitals in another column. Click the "Add-ons" tab, then "Flippity," and select "Flippity URL." Your students will now have a live flashcard link to access and share for studying.

Flippity
offered by sites.google.com/site/edlisten
Easily turn a Google™ Spreadsheet into a Set of Online Flashcards and Other Cool Stuff.

Image 8.1 Google and the Google logo are registered trademarks of Google Inc., used with permission.

SCHOOL: Use the Save as Doc Add-on to transfer information on a Google Sheet to a Google Doc. Sometimes information on a spreadsheet can be too difficult to read. Copying and pasting the information from one location to another can be clumsy at best. With the Save as Doc Add-on you can move parts of a spreadsheet to a Google Doc with a few clicks of the mouse. For example, if you are collecting information on a student to determine whether he or she qualifies for a support program, you can take teacher-submitted information from the Google Sheet and organize it on a reader-friendly Google Doc. Make sure to pay close attention to who has access to the documents if they are private in nature.

The first step you will take is to highlight the information you want transferred to the Google Doc. Then, once you have the Add-on downloaded, click on the "Add-ons" tab and select "Save as Doc." A box will appear on the right-hand side and provide you with a series of options. The next step you want to take is titling the Google Doc so it's easy to find later. Determine if you want the same headings that are on your spreadsheet to appear on the Google Doc. Finally, click the "Save as Doc" button at the bottom of the box. A Google Doc will then be generated and backed up to your Drive.

DISTRICT: **Enable the ezNotifications Google Sheets Add-on so that you receive notifications any time a Google Sheet is updated.** During the extreme time constraints of budget season, a number of central office people may be inputting numbers for next year's budget. Shared spreadsheets promote collaboration and efficiency. Sometimes though, it's unclear when people have updated various parts of the spreadsheet. By using the ezNotifications Google Sheet Add-on, multiple users know when people are working on certain parts of a spreadsheet. This Add-on can also be used when gathering information on students so you'll be notified as soon as possible.

Once the Add-on is downloaded in the Sheet you are working on, make it active by clicking on the "Add-ons" tab

> and selecting "ezNotifications." A box will appear on the right-hand side of the page, assisting you to set up spreadsheet notification. You can set notifications by hour or by day and allow editors of the spreadsheet to receive the notifications.

Google Sheets Add-ons provide Google Sheets aficionados with a tool chest full of hacks that will make life much easier. Don't be afraid to let students experiment with the Add-ons. They'll find many wonderful possibilities to extend their learning experiences in various subject areas. Take a moment and pilot one of the Add-ons mentioned in this chapter and see what it's capable of doing. Once you become comfortable with certain Add-ons, make sure to share your wealth of knowledge with someone else.

PROVIDE FEEDBACK IN SECONDS WITH FORMS

THE PROBLEM: HOW CAN WE GAIN INSTANT FEEDBACK FROM OUR STUDENTS OR STAFF?

A SOCIAL STUDIES TEACHER needed a quick way to end a lesson on the Civil War and gauge student understanding. Rather than passing out the dreaded paper exit slip, the teacher instructed students to open their devices, click on a link, and answer one simple multiple choice question. Instantly, she had feedback on the day's lesson—all through Google Forms.

Teachers can waste valuable class time gathering feedback through paper evaluations like exit slips. Five minutes of a forty-three-minute lesson is a lot of time, and one sheet of paper per student per class period is a lot of wasted paper. There's an easier way to get feedback from students and get it quickly without going through a stack of papers. The district wants to go paperless, so it might be better to find an alternative to an exit slip for gathering evidence of learning. While teachers grapple with these issues, administrators also face roadblocks in the quest to save time and resources. With all the surveys

> **Think of Google Forms as an online survey tool that interacts with other G Suite applications such as Google Sheets to make collaboration and data collection easy.**

they are asked to perform, they'd like to eliminate those hard copy handouts while still collecting data efficiently. Google Forms offers solutions to all of these problems.

THE HACK: USE GOOGLE FORMS FOR FEEDBACK

To access Google Forms, go to your Drive and click "New" then go down to "More" and go over to "Forms." Forms will open in a new tab. You will be able to add questions, type a name, and change the color of the Form. See Image 9.1 for the Forms icon.

Image 9.1 Google and the Google logo are registered trademarks of Google Inc., used with permission.

Google Forms allows for instant feedback from various stakeholders in a school district. Through Forms, a user can create questions and have the respondent answer in a variety of formats. Users can analyze and organize data in real time, get answers fast, and work with various school buildings to gain knowledge about technology integration. Think of Google Forms as an online survey tool that interacts with other G Suite applications such as Google Sheets to make collaboration and data collection easy. Google Forms is similar to SurveyMonkey, Poll Everywhere, and other online survey tools, but it is already included in G Suite, and you do not need to purchase any additional software.

Just a little note: Never manually input data in the Sheets file created for your Form until the Form is closed. Entering data manually while the Form is open will make the Add-ons function improperly.

What
YOU
Can Do Tomorrow

CLASSROOM: Create a Form to use at the beginning and end of a lesson. At the start of the lesson have students answer a simple multiple choice question to assess understanding of yesterday's concepts. At the end of the lesson have students scan a QR code or go to a website that brings them directly to a Google Form that serves as an exit slip or exit ticket. Google Forms allows you to choose the question style that works best for your class needs—a scale to rate understanding, multiple choice questions, or short responses.

Students can fill out the Form without needing to sign in to their own accounts, and you instantly get their feedback. The data appears either as individual responses or as a summary in Google Forms, and you can also view the information in Google Sheets. Depending on the question style, Google Forms displays the results in graphs, percentages, charts, or words.

SCHOOL: Create a survey using Forms and use your school's email list to send it to your stakeholders electronically. If your school does not have a parent email list set up yet, you can easily collect emails and create a list in Google Sheets. Gathering this type of information is helpful at the start of the school year to collate your parents' contact information. Next, set a deadline for survey responses. When the survey closes, you can view, save, and share response data electronically to cut down on paper. Feedback is instant, and you will be able to review the data in different ways, such as through a graph or individual responses.

DISTRICT: Create a Form for community members to register for a district event. Forms can be tailored to appeal to those attending the event with a custom background. Responses allow those holding the event to prepare for the number of people attending, which is especially beneficial when you want participation from those attending.

Scott used a Google Form to organize a community

technology night featuring different interactive stations. Sending out a Form prior to the event to have stakeholders register for the event ensured that stations were geared toward engaging everyone present. As an extra bonus, add a question on the Form for participants to leave their email addresses. After the event, use Forms to distribute a survey to those addresses. The survey empowers participants to express their feelings on the event and make suggestions for future community presentations.

Forms allows instant feedback from the classroom, school, or district. A Form's quick and easy setup allows for immediate data collection. Engagement will increase as you respond to the results of data quickly.

ELEVATE YOUR FEEDBACK METHODS WITH FORMS ADD-ONS

THE PROBLEM: FEEDBACK OR INPUT TAKES TOO LONG

Teacher ADAM SCHOENBART from Ossining, New York, wanted to be able to automate the grading and feedback process from Google Forms. Students need feedback, and he wanted to be better at providing it. He turned to Add-ons to enhance the power of Forms and Sheets. Using Flubaroo for Google Sheets, he was able to grade a Google Forms quiz and share scores and feedback instantly. Adam and his students knew more about their learning: Add-ons made it easier for everyone.

Forms Add-ons help not only classrooms, but also staff settings and beyond. Billy, who worked in NJASCD North Region, found that educators would want their professional development certificates as proof that they had attended an event. It could take hours to make sure that all of the names were collected and that people had actually been present. Then, Natalie Franzi, the secretary of NJASCD North at that time, had an easy solution to get certificates to educators quickly: It was just a matter of adding autoCrat to the feedback survey that educators filled out at the end of an event.

> The short amount of time you spend putting Add-ons into action will pay off in their power to organize and generate information.

THE HACK: USE GOOGLE FORMS FOR FEEDBACK

Just as with Sheets and Docs, a number of different Add-ons enhance Forms. Add-ons can be applied easily by opening up a new Google Form in Drive and clicking the three little dots in the upper right-hand corner of the screen. Then, click "Add-ons" and select the Add-ons you want to use. Once you upload the Add-on, it can be activated by clicking the puzzle piece icon at the top of the screen. Certain Add-ons in Forms provide instant emails to people once they have filled out a Form. Other Add-ons like g(Math) for Forms allow users to embed graphs and equations directly into a Form. There are many other different Add-ons that can be used to enhance your experience with Forms. These enhancements allow Forms to become much more than just a place to collect data.

What YOU Can Do Tomorrow

CLASSROOM: Flubaroo provides immediate results and feedback for quizzes on Google Forms. With this Add-on, students know more about their learning progress and how to improve. The teacher creates a Google Forms quiz, generates an answer key by taking the quiz, and then Flubaroo grades the quiz by comparing student responses to the teacher key. It's best for multiple choice questions, but it also allows for open-ended responses. While Google Forms now has a basic quiz feature, Flubaroo provides more detail and insight into student learning and growth. It also provides valuable feedback to the teacher about low-scoring questions, student progress, and more.

SCHOOL: Use the g(Math) for Forms Add-on to conduct digital formative assessments that can drive math instruction decisions in your building. This Add-on will allow math teachers to create short or lengthy assessments that include embedded graphs and equations. See Image 10.1 for a look at

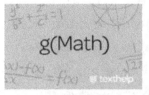

the Add-on. Once administered, the data linked to these Google Forms assessments can be viewed in the "Summary of Responses" area in Forms or Sheets. Remember, any time you create a Google Form the data can be linked to a Google

Image 10.1 Google and the Google logo are registered trademarks of Google Inc., used with permission.

Sheet. Data-driven discussions can take place at subject-area or grade-level meetings.

DISTRICT: Use autoCrat to generate professional development certificates immediately following your staff's next training. Note that autoCrat is an Add-on in Sheets, but it pulls data from Forms. If you plan to use autoCrat, make sure to leave a space for people's first and last names along with their emails on the Form. When Natalie Franzi was secretary of NJASCD North, she created these steps to generate a professional development certificate through autoCrat. While reading through these steps, it would be helpful to be sitting in front of your computer to practice.

First you need to create a certificate for the professional development event. You can create a template in Google Docs. When you are creating the certificate, make sure to add merge tags for any data, such as people's names, that will be filled in from the Form. The information from the Form needs to match the tags in the Google Doc. An example of the tag would be <<First Name>> <<Last

Name>> on the Form. You do not need the << >>. You just need them as a placeholder in the Doc.

Use Google Forms to create your survey. Be sure to include questions that will collect the information for your merge tags. In your Google Drive, a second file will automatically be created that is a Google Sheet. Your responses get recorded on this Sheet. Select "Add-ons" and install "autoCrat." See Image 10.2 for the autoCrat icon. Follow the autoCrat directions to set up your Merge Job. First, you will need to name the Merge Job. For example, give the job the name of the conference and the person's first and last name. autoCrat will automatically create a folder in your Drive for the merged Doc to be stored.

Image 10.2 Google and the Google logo are registered trademarks of Google Inc., used with permission.

Use "File naming convention" for the value of Last Name and the name of the conference. This will create a new file. Select PDF for document type so the certificate cannot be modified. Check the box for "Email and/or share merged documents," use the value for email in the "To" field. Create your subject and message for your participants to receive. Then click on "Advanced Settings." Check off "Run autoCrat when new form is submitted." If you would like your Form automatically sent once your responses are collected, select "Run Merge" to have your certificates emailed.

Try these steps to create your own automatic professional development certificate with autoCrat Add-on.

Forms Add-ons enhance feedback in classrooms, schools, and districts. If some of the options we've suggested seem overwhelming, give them a try. They're not as intimidating as they may seem at first glance. The short amount of time you spend putting Add-ons into action will pay off in their power to organize and generate information.

HACK 11

ENGAGE YOUR AUDIENCE WITH SLIDES

THE PROBLEM: PRESENTATIONS LACK CLARITY

IN LOOKING BACK at past workshops he has attended, Brad clearly remembers a session titled PowerPointless. The presenter spoke about the ineffective ways that people use multimedia programs such as PowerPoint to engage an audience. Meaningful messages got undercut by too many images, paragraphs of information, and annoying sound effects. All of these bad habits sounded familiar. Brad had seen students and educators disengage audiences with ineffective multimedia presentations far too often.

The presenter suggested ways to sidestep these bad habits and keep multimedia presentations straightforward: They should consist of one or two eye-appealing images and be limited to five words per line and five lines per slide. Brad conveyed these important suggestions to his students in his computer application class as they created their very own PowerPoint presentations.

Fast forward to the present: Brad is now a school leader and national presenter who uses Google Slides in the same fashion that he implored his former students to use PowerPoint. Google Slides has major advantages over other multimedia programs. For starters, Google Slides

> **Google Slides enhances learning, teaching, leadership, and presentations.**

is web-based and links to your Google account. Users do not have to worry about clicking the "save" button, because changes take effect automatically and multiple users can collaborate on a slide deck in real time. Students, teachers, and administrators can make Google Slides work for them in many ways.

THE HACK: ENGAGE AUDIENCES WITH GOOGLE SLIDES

Open up your Chrome browser, click on the waffle in the upper right-hand corner, and locate the yellow "Google Slides" icon. Once inside the document, you should familiarize yourself with the many features. To start building your slide deck you will want to add slides, either by clicking the "+" sign on the upper left-hand corner of the screen or by clicking the "Slide" tab and selecting the "New slide" option. From this point you can change the theme of the entire presentation, adjust layouts for individual slides, and add information.

Features in Slides can move your presentation from good to great. The Q&A feature allows the audience to post questions on the shared slide deck. Click on the scroll-down arrow next to the "Present" button in the upper right-hand corner of the screen. Select the "Presenter view" option, which will push out the Q&A feature. You will notice that a link appears at the top of your slide that provides audience members an opportunity to ask questions during the presentation. You will be notified when a question is asked, or you can simply click on "Presenter View" to see the questions that the audience submits.

The Explore feature allows users to search for information on the web, change templates for specific slides, and do a variety of other things. Activate it by clicking on the "Explore" button in the lower right-hand corner of the slide. You can also publish your presentation to the web using a link or embedded code. Go to "File" and then "Publish on the web" to see the various publishing options.

What YOU Can Do Tomorrow

CLASSROOM: Empower students to show what they know about a topic by crowdsourcing a Google Slide presentation. Imagine teaching elementary, middle, or high school science students about the impact weather has on our lives. Individuals or groups of students could tackle a specific sub-topic within the broader concept of weather. Each team would be responsible for sharing their research findings on one slide. Put all the slides together to create a Google Slide presentation that encompasses the key concepts related to weather. The teacher can share the slide deck with the entire class by posting in Google Classroom or by projecting it on an interactive whiteboard. The presentation can also be a valuable resource to share with other grade levels or future students.

SCHOOL: Disseminate information to stakeholders about an important issue like standardized testing or online safety. Schools often hold parent presentations to share insight on matters related to curriculum, standardized testing, bullying, or online safety. Unfortunately, many parents are unable to attend these presentations. Take advantage of the ability to embed or share a slide deck in Google Slides so parents can read it at their own leisure. Embed the Slide presentation onto your school website or share the link in the virtual school newsletter.

DISTRICT: Collaborate on a district-wide committee presentation in real time with Google Slides. District-wide committees that span various stakeholder groups may be tasked with creating presentations to highlight initiatives. Due to everyone's crazy schedules it's sometimes impossible to meet in the physical world. Google Slides allows multiple people to access and collaborate in the virtual world.

For example, you might be a member of a committee that is looking to revamp certain learning spaces throughout the district. The committee has set goals, conducted research, established a budget, and made site visits throughout the state. Now it's time to present findings to the board of education for final approval. One member creates a Google Slide presentation, giving editing rights to all of the committee members. Each person is designated one or two slides relating to various parts of the initiative. Over the next few weeks, members collaborate on the virtual slide deck and use the comment and chat features for feedback and editing purposes. On the night of the board meeting, the presentation can be pushed out through Chromecast to a large flat-panel screen in the room (see Hack 18). In addition, the committee posts the Google Slide presentation to the board of education webpage for the public to view at a later date.

Google Slides enhances learning, teaching, leadership, and presentations. Its users have opportunities to collaborate and share stories in both the physical and virtual worlds. Furthermore, its virtual interaction components allow people to provide their unique contributions. As with any other tool, careful modeling will allow students to understand its capabilities. To learn its various possibilities yourself, start small and collaborate on a Google Slide project with a colleague or friend. Understand its potential: With thoughtful use, it can shift a message from being merely useful to being transformative.

HACK 12

THINK OUTSIDE THE BOX WITH GOOGLE CLASSROOM

THE PROBLEM: HOW CAN STUDENTS, TEACHERS, AND ADMINISTRATORS WORK SMARTER AND NOT HARDER?

CHRISSY ROMANO-ARRABITO, A teacher in Hackensack, New Jersey, drowned in paperwork while teaching middle school English with a roster of over 100 students. Like many teachers, she spent countless hours providing feedback, grading papers, responding to emails, and sitting through boring staff meetings. She knew she needed to find a way to make better use of her time, streamline her workflow, and keep her students engaged in their learning experiences. She works in a G Suite district, so when Google Classroom was rolled out in 2014 she knew she had to give it a try.

Chrissy quickly learned how to push out assignments and provide feedback to ease her workflow. As Google Classroom evolved, so did her creativity. She not only found ways to make this platform engaging for her students, but she also realized ways to use Classroom at the school and district levels. Once you see how its features

> **This Drive management system brings together all the features of G Suite into one easy-to-use platform, allowing you to connect with students or staff members.**

can stir creative juices for any Google user, you may wish to promote the platform to your district if you do not have access to it at present.

THE HACK: THINK OUTSIDE THE BOX FOR MORE CREATIVE AND UNCONVENTIONAL USES

Google Classroom is incredibly intuitive. The Stream, a key feature of Classroom, is similar to the news feed you might encounter in other social media platforms. It acts as the communication pulse and organizational center for your Classroom. Stream tools, such as the + sign, allow teachers to add information, announcements, and assignments, and its calendar feature can be leveraged for scheduling and due dates.

When students post to the Stream, they choose whether to share work publicly for the whole class or privately for just the teacher. If they wish to share their work with the teacher, they click the "ADD" button to select a file, either from their Drive or from an external source such as a 60-second video, a voice memo, a digital representation of their sketchnotes, a slide presentation, or a music playlist. As long as students use a Chromebook, smartphone, or laptop to capture video and images, they can upload the work to Classroom. Students may also post links to their blogs or websites. Students may also click on "CREATE" and begin working right then and there in Docs, Slides, Sheets, or Drawings to show what they know.

As part of G Suite for Education, your Classroom also has access to a Google Voice number. Take advantage of Voice in the classroom to foster an atmosphere of open communication and to boost efficiency in offering feedback. You can post your telephone number and the hours you will be available on Voice in the About section of your Classroom. The further beauty of Google Voice is that it will transcribe a voicemail to an email or text message for easy accessibility. You can listen to student messages and post your response to the Stream in Classroom. Chances are that if one student has a question, others are confused as well, so posting in the Stream makes the information accessible to all. Make sure you explain this to students in advance so they are not expecting you to pick up the phone or call them back (unless of course you want to). Tell them that once they leave the message, you will respond within a certain time frame in the Classroom Stream.

If you would prefer to hold "office hours" similar to what one would experience in a higher education setting, Classroom makes that easy, too. You simply create a permanent link to a Google Hangout and post the link in the About section of your Classroom. Students can then click on the link during your prescribed "office hours" to reach you virtually. This is an excellent alternative for students who rely on a bus to get to and from school and cannot arrange for early arrival or late pick up.

What
YOU
Can Do Tomorrow

CLASSROOM: Make learning fun with Voki. Classroom has a host of tools that open up possibilities for communication and innovation. For example, Voki allows you to incorporate talking avatars into your Classroom. You can use Voki to present directions and make announcements that you would otherwise type into the Classroom Stream, and once you master Voki basics, you can get really creative. The avatars can be used in an ELA class as an innovative way for students to talk through what they know in lieu of the traditional essay, report, or slide presentation. They can also be used as a digital storytelling tool. In a social studies class, students could create a Voki to bring historical figures to life. Integrating Voki is easy: Once you have created the avatar you simply copy and paste the link into the Stream with the "Add" button. There are two versions of Voki: a free version that has your basic features and a version that has a cost associated with premium features.

SCHOOL: Ditch the traditional staff meeting. Some schools have transformed staff meetings into EdCamp-style gatherings, leaving the housekeeping items to be disseminated via Google Classroom. For example, the Create Question feature allows for building leaders to ask questions and gather information from staff in a timely manner. Use the "+" button to add your question to the Stream. Before you click "POST" you have the option to allow "students," in this case teachers and other staff, to see each other's responses and reply to each other's posts. You can also give them the option to edit their answers after they submit them. Before a staff meeting or a professional development session, a building leader can ask staff members what they are interested in learning about or what concerns they would like to discuss.

DISTRICT: Keep all your ducks in a row. It is quite common for an email to get overlooked or an interoffice envelope to go missing. The Classroom platform allows central office personnel to keep track of data from each school in the district. The superintendent can create the Classroom and invite other central office staff as "teachers" so they are privy to any information that is submitted. Building leaders would join as "students" and turn in budgets, incident reports, or other documents via Classroom.

Classroom may also be used for district-wide committees. For example, the Digital Learning Committee in Chrissy's district is comprised of staff from all of the six schools along with central office personnel. The Director of Technology created the Classroom and added the committee members as "students." This Classroom has become an easily accessible central repository for resources and information.

Google Classroom is a game-changer in education. It provides people with an opportunity to work and learn in a paperless environment. Google Classroom can help drive change, enhance communication efforts, promote collaboration, and inspire thinking. Make it a part of your learning environment today and see students thrive in ways that would once have been unimaginable. This Drive management system brings together all the features of G Suite into one easy-to-use platform, allowing you to connect with students or staff members. Google Classroom is also available to anyone with a personal Google account. This means that people have access to many of the same Google Classroom features that are available to educators in G Suite for Education school districts.

HACK 13

KEEP IT IN ONE PLACE

THE PROBLEM: ORGANIZING IDEAS, THOUGHTS, AND TASKS

Have you ever used multiple sticky notes, papers, and backs of envelopes to keep track of tasks and ideas that pop into your head? If you are like us, the answer is yes. Like us, you may think to yourself, "That doesn't work." The problem is that when we are on the go or at our desks, we grab the closest scrap of paper or sticky note to write down an idea, message, or thought, and then we shove it aside. When we need it, we can't remember where that note went.

Disorganized note-making feels confusing and distracting. When Scott develops administrative meeting agendas for his Monday morning meetings, he avoids the clutter with Google Keep. Not only is Keep a valuable way to organize, but it can also boost collaboration and help prevent oversights.

> **Keep permits putting multiple notes in one window: Add pictures, make drawings, and create checklists for students to use.**

THE HACK: GOOGLE KEEP ORGANIZES ALL YOUR THOUGHTS IN ONE PLACE

Google Keep, which can be used on any device that supports Google products, allows users to quickly jot down thoughts so they can organize ideas in ways that make sense. Your thoughts can then be shared with others. Keep permits putting multiple notes in one window: Add pictures, make drawings, and create checklists for students to use. As part of the G Suite family, Keep allows you to drag and drop notes, checklists, or images into your Google Docs, making interaction on the go easier. See an example of what Keep can do in Image 13.1.

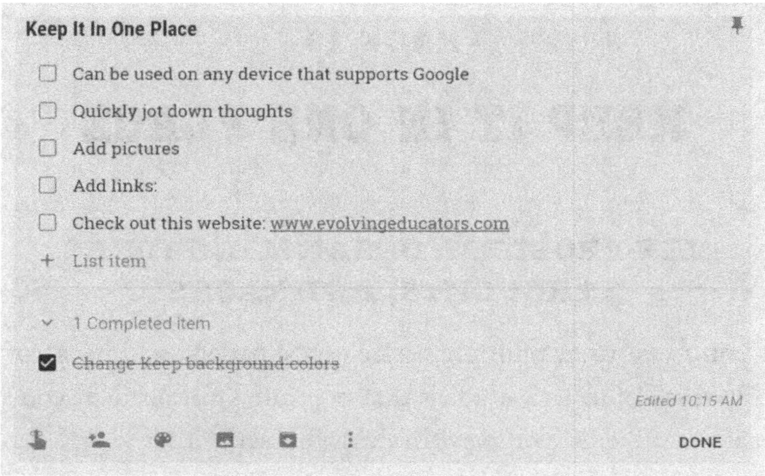

Image 13.1 Google and the Google logo are registered trademarks of Google Inc., used with permission.

You can find Google Keep on your computer by opening Chrome and clicking on the waffle on the top right. Click on "More" at the bottom of the drop-down screen, then click "Even more from Google" at the bottom of the next drop-down screen. Go to the section labeled "Organize your stuff" and click on "Keep." It's important to note that you can also download it to your phone through the App Store (see more on that in Hack 20).

Once you have the app you can get started by clicking the yellow icon that has the light bulb in the center. When it opens, you start typing in the "Take a note" section. From there, a whole range of features is open to you.

What YOU Can Do Tomorrow

CLASSROOM: Create a writer's checklist for students.

Teachers can create a writer's checklist for students and share it with them. The students then use it by marking off the checkboxes throughout the writing process. Creating a list in Keep is easy: Open the app in Chrome. Type the first step of your writer's checklist in the section that says "Take a note." This will open up a new note. Press enter to go to the next line, add a title in the area labeled "Title." Add as many steps as you want to the checklist. To delete an item, just scroll over it and an "X" will show up on the right side. Click it and the item is removed.

Now we need to make it a real checklist. On the bottom there are a number of symbols. Click the three dots on the right. Click "Show checkboxes" in the drop-down menu. Now students can check off each step as they complete it.

When students check a box it will go to the bottom of the list and strike it out. If you do not want the completed items to move, change this feature by clicking on the "Settings" gear on the left side of the screen and the menu will come up. Unclick the checkbox labeled "Move checked items to bottom."

Bonus: The teacher can download the checklist to Docs to grade the students' work based on the checklist. This Doc is then shared with the students when the assignment has been graded. See the District Hack below to find out how.

SCHOOL: Create an inviting faculty meeting agenda with an image, topics for discussion, and links for additional information. Principals can create a faculty meeting agenda for their schools with images and links to additional information. Just follow the steps above to create an agenda list with or without checkboxes. Add an image to the top by clicking on the fourth symbol on the bottom of the list—it looks like a picture. You will then be able to select an image file. If later you decide you don't like the image, scroll over it with your cursor and move it to the trash can that will show up on the bottom right of the image section.

Type in link addresses or copy and paste a web address to add links to the agenda. You can also write information and then include the address in the message. For example, you can add the statement: Check out the website www.evolvingeducators.com, and once you type the website or link to the address it will automatically become an active link, turn blue, and be underlined. See Image 13.2 for an example. As of this publication you cannot add embedded links.

Image 13.2 Google and the Google logo are registered trademarks of Google Inc., used with permission.

DISTRICT: Create meeting minutes by downloading or dragging your Google Keep agenda to Google Docs. For a meeting to be memorialized, the agenda and discussion must be turned into minutes. Scott schedules meeting participants to take turns at note-taking in his Monday morning meetings. Instead of reinventing the whole agenda by retyping it in Docs, and filling in the notes, they use the Keep agenda that they download into Docs. The person then assigned to note-taking that day will take notes and share them in a common Drive folder with everyone in the meeting.

> Remove myself
>
> Add label
>
> Make a copy
>
> Report abuse
>
> Copy to Google Doc

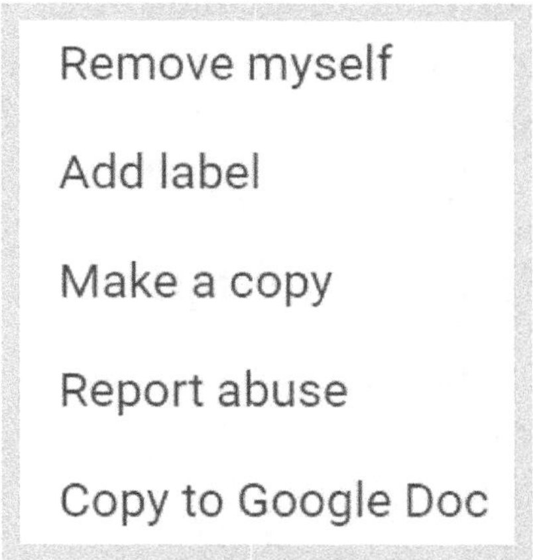

Image 13.3 Google and the Google logo are registered trademarks of Google Inc., used with permission.

The Keep agenda may be downloaded to Docs by first clicking the three dots at the bottom of the agenda and then clicking on "Copy to Google Doc." Open your Drive and open the Doc that is now saved there with the title you gave the Keep note. You can start taking notes immediately, and share the Doc with everyone in the meeting. See Image 13.3 for the "Copy to Google Doc" location.

Bonus: Keep allows you to share the list you develop by clicking on the second symbol on the bottom, which is a "+" and person symbol. This opens another screen to start adding people you want to share with. Click "Save" when you're done.

Google Keep is a gem of an app that offers many features that are useful to the classroom, school, and district. We hit on just a few of these. We encourage you to explore it and find more features that you can use in your role as an educator.

ORGANIZE AND SHARE YOUR THOUGHTS VIRTUALLY WITH DRAWINGS

THE PROBLEM: INFORMATION IS OFTEN PORTRAYED IN A MESSY AND CONFUSING FASHION

A T SOME POINT in your lifetime you probably have come across long, drawn-out information in a handout or presentation. You probably said to your-self, "If I were in charge of putting together this presentation or set of notes, I would have some sort of graphic organizer or visual that's easy on the eyes."

Teachers introduce graphic organizers so their classes can break down content into simpler terms. It may be a Venn diagram to compare and contrast, or it may be a timeline to put events in chronological order. Administrators often choose flowcharts and mind maps to clarify important information for an audience. People respond to and learn from visuals, sometimes even more than from your run-of-the-mill report or slide deck.

> Using the Drawings program's tools, you can create your own graphic organizers or use a template that someone has made available on the web.

THE HACK: CREATE GRAPHIC ORGANIZERS WITH GOOGLE DRAWINGS

Leverage the power of Google Drawings to create organizers that enhance learning experiences for students and disseminate information to staff. To get started, access Drive from the waffle and click the "New" button on the left-hand side of the page. Then scroll down until you see the "Drawings" option. Once in Drawings you will notice many similarities between the setup of this application and the setup of Docs and Slides.

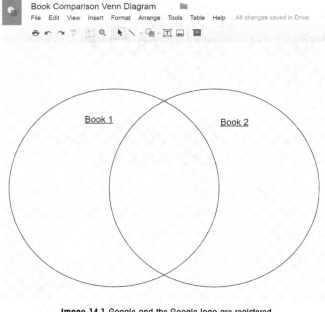

Image 14.1 Google and the Google logo are registered trademarks of Google Inc., used with permission.

Using the Drawings program's tools, you can create your own graphic organizers or use a template that someone has made available on the web. Better yet, click on "Tools" at the top of the Drawings document, and click "Explore." You will see a search box appear on the right-hand side of your screen. From there you can search for templates. All you need to do is click on the link provided by the creator of the document to access your very own copy.

Looking to create your own graphic organizer or diagram? You can do this in Google Drawings or in an application like Google Docs. Let's use the Google Drawings feature inside of Google Docs as an example. Look to the top of the screen and click on the "Insert" tab. From there, you can select different lines, shapes, charts, and other features to enhance your document. To move the object you created to different parts of the document, simply click on the "Arrange" tab to see the various available options. You can also share and collaborate on the Google Drawings document with another user by clicking on the "Share" button in the upper right-hand corner of the screen. Look at Image 14.1 to see an example of a Venn diagram, which was created in Google Drawings, that compares and contrasts two books.

What
YOU
Can Do Tomorrow

CLASSROOM: Design a graphic organizer that helps students break down a topic. There are so many different types of graphic organizers that you or your students can create to help with making sense of the topic. These include KWL charts, Venn diagrams, character maps, and plot diagrams, to name a few. Create or modify existing Google Drawings documents to serve your purpose. A useful technique would be to give students time in class to examine exemplar graphic organizers and then create their very own.

SCHOOL: Use Google Drawings to facilitate professional learning. Conduct a faculty meeting activity by placing staff members in groups and task them with breaking down an article on a best practice teaching technique. Give each group a Google Drawings mind map that is to be completed and shared with the rest of the faculty for further discussion. The mind map can be mirrored to the SMART Board or projector in the room through the Google Cast extension. Further discussion can take place with the entire faculty about each group's findings.

DISTRICT: Create flowcharts for the various departments and organizational structures that exist throughout the district. Once the flowcharts are complete they can be disseminated to appropriate personnel and updated in real time

> whenever changes occur. For example, your district might be changing the structure of the Crisis Management Team. This important information needs to be captured in a visually compelling way so that people understand their roles in the unfortunate circumstance that a crisis does happen.

Google Drawings provides users at the classroom, school, and district levels opportunities to display information in a clear and efficient manner. It's important to remember that stakeholders need training and time to figure out how Google Drawings, or any tool for that matter, can work for them. Google Apps like Drawings do not have to be developed in isolation: The various sharing features and commenting abilities allow users to collaborate in real time to create a product that enhances learning.

HACK 15

NARROW DOWN YOUR GOOGLE SEARCH RESULTS

THE PROBLEM: GOOGLE SEARCHES DO NOT PRODUCE THE RESULTS YOU NEED

Internet searches provide a laundry list of results that include links to sites, articles, and research. They also produce news, images, and other less useful results. Many of those results do not relate to the topic you are searching. Even though millions of images might pop up in a search feed, any images you want to use must include proper copyright permissions. Nor are all the results appropriate for student use: We have all heard the horror stories of teachers assigning a search and inappropriate content coming up in the search results. As educators in New Jersey, we've even lived out the horror ourselves a few times. For example, when you search the New Jersey state bird in Google Images, often times you will get a few images of the middle finger. (As native New Jerseyans, we don't find this that funny, but those of you with preconceived notions of what "Jersey" is all about might think it is correct!)

Fortunately, these mix-ups do not have to happen, and we can focus our student searches for better results. We can, as Billy does in his computer classes, teach our students responsible usage and emphasize that what comes across our screens may not always be appropriate for school. We can also teach students to apply search filters to minimize the occurrence of inappropriate

> By teaching students to focus their research you will provide them with a life skill that goes beyond hitting the search button.

images, and ensure that students are following proper rights and permissions rules for the information they find.

Not only do these filters come in handy in the classroom, they also benefit school-wide and district goals. For instance, Scott's social media strategy for his district includes using images in Tweets and Facebook posts for school announcements, activities, and events. People like a visual alongside information, and a tasteful use of images boosts professional appeal. When finding images, Scott always filters those searches to find appropriate image rights so there is no copyright infringement. Check out our chapter on Google extensions on how to capture an image and edit it.

THE HACK: USE THE SETTINGS AND TOOLS FEATURES IN GOOGLE SEARCH

The settings and tools features in Google Search, which are located below the search bar, allow teachers, school administrators, and district administration to refine, limit, and focus research through Google. By using all the settings and tools Google Search has to offer, you maximize results, become more effective in your search, and have more time for the work you need to com-

Image 15.1 Google and the Google logo are registered trademarks of Google Inc., used with permission.

plete because you find useful results. By clicking on the "Settings" or "Tools" button, you will be given a variety of options to explore. Each creates a better search experience for you and your students. See Image 15.1 for a look at the locations of "Settings" and "Tools."

What YOU Can Do Tomorrow

CLASSROOM: Focus student research through key search settings. Every good lesson and project teaches students skills that they can use now and in the future. By teaching students to focus their research, you will provide them with a life skill that goes beyond hitting the search button. You can start in the search settings by limiting or increasing the number of search results available per page. Click on the "Settings" button below the search bar, then click "Search settings." Review the options available in the section that identifies how many results per page. Just slide the box to the number you want. See Image 15.2 for a view of the slide.

Results per page

Google Instant shows 10 results

10   20   30   40   50   100
Faster   Slower

Image 15.2 Google and the Google logo are registered trademarks of Google Inc., used with permission.

Limit the number of results based on the age and skill level of your students. Fewer results per page allow students to focus on the results in front of them. More results per page allow students to use their skills to evaluate the best results from those provided.

Either way, students will need to open search results to review the content. It may be beneficial to set the search results to open in a separate window when they are selected. This allows students to flip through tabs instead of continually hitting the back arrow to find something they liked. Finally, you can set the "SafeSearch" filter in the search settings to block inappropriate language and images.

SCHOOL: Sort images in Google Search by image rights. One of the most valuable communication tools a school can use is social media. To make a post more appealing, many schools include images, both those they have taken on their own and those from a search on Google. Some people do not realize that many images are copyrighted and so have specific limits for their use. Google makes finding appropriate images easy with its Advanced Search settings. Choosing the correct image rights gives a district permission rights to use searched images and modify them for school use in an appropriate way. You can access Advanced Search settings by clicking on "Settings," then clicking on "Advanced Search," where a new tab will open up and give you many options to choose from. See image 15.3 below. One of those options, at the bottom, is "usage rights." Click on it and you will get a drop-down menu to select the usage rights for your image.

Image 15.3 Google and the Google logo are registered trademarks of Google Inc., used with permission.

DISTRICT: Set a range of time to filter results and search verbatim with the Tools feature. Districts have a vital need to get updated or recent search results on various educational topics or on news stories related to their own district. Filtering your search results in Google Search Tools will accomplish this by

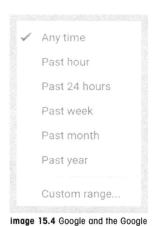

Image 15.4 Google and the Google logo are registered trademarks of Google Inc., used with permission.

searching a topic through six preset time ranges or in a custom time range. This feature allows you to track the history of an educational topic.

You can also search verbatim so that you get no variations to your search term. Districts will find this useful when finding a key term or specific educational verbiage without similar term results. To apply these filters, click on "Tools" below your search box. Using the "Any time" tab, click on the downward triangle and select a preset range of times, or establish your own range by clicking on the "Custom range" button at the bottom. See Image 15.4 for a view of the tab. Using the "All results" button to the right of the "Any time" button, you can select the type of results you want, from all results to verbatim.

We waste so much time with unstructured Google searches—that time can be better spent reviewing focused search content. Taking steps to improve our ability to search on Google will focus our students and provide appropriate content, allow us to use images with the correct image rights, and search information for specific time frames or by exact wording. These hacks improve our ability to find the specific information we need for classrooms, schools, and districts, so use the settings or tools features to dig deeper and more accurately into your educational searches.

HACK 16

MONITOR THE WEB WITH GOOGLE ALERTS

THE PROBLEM: PEOPLE HAVE NO IDEA WHEN SOMETHING THEY ARE ASSOCIATED WITH IS MENTIONED ONLINE

THE INTERNET HAS too much information to sift through. As a case in point, try Googling the word "alert." We got over 715,000,000 search results. Who has time to go through that many results? In this age of digital information and social media, it's imperative that teachers, principals, and superintendents stay current with the school-specific information that is out there on the internet. For the most part, the days of clipping out articles from local, state, or national newspapers are gone. Everything is posted online, which makes it difficult to keep track of news that might highlight or mention you or your district.

In addition to monitoring their digital presence, people need a place to store and display the content digitally. There's no limit to the great district events you can promote, especially through a Twitter feed, Facebook page, or Pinterest board. Promotion obviously starts with having the information to share in the first place.

> **Teachers can have students use Alerts as a research tool for a project. Principals can use it as a way to tell their school's story. District search committees can use Alerts to research their next superintendent.**

The best way to track information on the web in a timely fashion is through a little-known feature called Google Alerts.

THE HACK: ACTIVATE GOOGLE ALERTS TO STAY NOTIFIED OF YOUR WEB PRESENCE

To get started, you can access Alerts by scanning the QR code in Image 16.1 or by typing www.google.com/alerts into your browser and following the instructions that are laid out below.

Image 16.1

Make sure that you are signed in to the correct Google account by using your Gmail account username and password. Scroll through the Google Alert homepage to become familiar with its various sections. You will notice that there are three sections starting from the top and working your way down the page: Search Box, My Alerts, and Alert Suggestions. Let's take a moment and learn how the Search Box works. Where it says "Create an alert about…" type in something that you would want an Alert about. For example, Brad Currie or Evolving Educators or #Satchat. Your selected searches will wind up in a feed just below the Search Box in a place called "My Alerts."

Explore the My Alerts area to understand how it functions. You will notice a gear in the upper right-hand corner. Click on it and you will see two options titled "Delivery Time" and "Digest." The "Delivery Time" feature provides you with an opportunity to select a time of the day that you want an Alert(s) to show up in your Gmail inbox. The "Digest" feature provides you with an opportunity to receive Alert(s) in a Gmail inbox of your choice on a daily or weekly basis.

Also browse the Alert Suggestions area. Maybe there are certain things that interest you, like Google Updates, that you want to stay on top of. If you select "Google Updates," you will receive a Gmail inbox Alert every time there is news mentioned pertaining to the topic called "Google Updates." Once selected it will give you an Alert preview and from this point you can choose to enable the Alert or not. The Alert Suggestions section enables you to quickly add Alerts pertaining to trending topics, organizations, or people. Click the "+" to add the item to your Alert feed. Click the garbage can icon next to the topic in the "My Alerts" section to stop receiving notifications. You can also click the unsubscribe link at the bottom of the Alert in your Gmail inbox.

What YOU Can Do Tomorrow

CLASSROOM: Students can use Alerts to research a particular person, place, or thing for a project. Say for example students are creating a Google Slide presentation on the life and achievements of Dr. Martin Luther King, Jr. They could set up an Alert for a one- or two-week period that will then push out content to their Gmail inboxes every time there is a newsworthy mention of Dr. King on the internet. This would be particularly useful around the time of Martin Luther King, Jr. Day when information on celebrations and programs is being disseminated. These Alerts can enhance opportunities for students to learn about him in class.

SCHOOL: Principals and teachers can keep track of school-related news by setting up an Alert. For example, Brad keeps track of all things Black River Middle School (BRMS) by setting up an Alert. Every time BRMS is mentioned in a newsworthy sort of way online he gets an Alert in his Gmail inbox. He will then push out these newsworthy links onto his school's Pinterest board, Twitter feed, and Facebook page. This is a great way to acknowledge and archive all the amazing things that are going on in your school. It also makes it very easy for school stakeholders to find important news items.

DISTRICT: School board members or a district-wide search team may want to keep track of candidates for a future superintendent opening. Once a list of candidates is compiled, Alerts can be set up for those specific people and the current schools they work for. Over the coming weeks and months, Alerts about news pertaining to the candidates will be sent to a specified Gmail inbox. Any items of interest can be forwarded to the decision-makers on the committee. It's a great way to collect artifacts to support informed decisions.

Google Alerts has many benefits for educators, but there are some negatives or obstacles associated with it. Your inbox could be flooded with alerts that have nothing to do with the topic you selected. There is more than one school with the same name. On rare occasions you could foreseeably receive an inappropriate alert that looks like spam. Overall, Google Alerts is well worth the investment. Teachers can have students use Alerts as a research tool for a project. Principals can use it as a way to tell their school's story. District search committees can use Alerts to research their next superintendent. It will save you time and pinpoint searchable topics for all to enjoy.

HACK 17

COMMIT TO CHROMEBOOKS

THE PROBLEM: DISTRICTS HAVE TOO MANY DEVICES TO MANAGE

MANY OF US have saved documents on the hard drives of our laptops or desktops. Gaining access to or sharing these documents required a memory stick, email, or floppy disk. This process took a long time, and documents often got lost in translation. Laptops are clunky and heavy, and for the longest time they needed to be hardwired to gain stable internet access. Desktop computers were always much more reliable, but mobility was always an issue. Over the past decade, strong Wi-Fi signals and robust infrastructures have given people the ability to move about freely with their devices and work more efficiently. This has enabled schools to support BYOD (Bring Your Own Device) and 1:1 environments. There are positives and negatives to both, but a system of 1:1 Chromebooks is cost effective and drives productivity in the virtual world.

> Chromebooks can benefit school districts by driving technology costs down, promoting cloud-based workflow, and providing an equal playing field for all stakeholders.

When students and staff juggle multiple devices, work becomes more complex. Technicians get overwhelmed with work orders and are sometimes unable to fix issues in-house. Routine procedural measures become disrupted. Lack of a common device or operating system due to different devices interferes with learning environments. On the flip side, BYOD environments provide students with an opportunity to work with devices that they are more comfortable with and take the burden off of districts to purchase devices for all students.

If your district uses G Suite for Education, it's a good idea to leverage the power of Chromebooks. What if your district hasn't yet fully committed to G Suite? You can always plan and budget for the transition of Googlifying your district in the near future. Students and staff could be steered toward purchasing their own Chromebooks, especially if your district has a Bring Your Own Device policy.

THE HACK: STICK WITH THE CHROMEBOOK TO EMPOWER STAKEHOLDERS

Commit to the Chromebook. A Chromebook runs off of the Google Chrome Operating System and operates when connected to the internet. Most of the apps and documents reside in the cloud. As long as you have access to Wi-Fi, you will be able to use your Chromebook anywhere in the world. Chromebooks are quite affordable and typically run somewhere around the $250 range. They work off of your personal or district-issued Google email account. Once the Chromebook is open, a prompt will appear asking you to log in with your Google email and password. You will notice the Chrome browser icon, which will drive your workflow. Click on the icon to start your cloud-based experience. For the most part, you cannot save work on the hard drive of the Chromebook. Again, it's important to point out that all document saving and communication is done in the cloud.

From an educational standpoint, here are some tips that will be helpful as you integrate Chromebooks into your environment:

- Purchase cases for all Chromebooks. Conduct a Google search with the Chromebook model number to find the appropriate case.

- Purchase charging carts for all Chromebooks. This will ensure Chromebooks are stored safely and charged at all times.

- Purchase insurance or extended warranties on the Chromebooks. Typically, parents pay a fee to protect their children's Chromebooks, which will help defray costs for districts. In other instances districts will pick up the tab if families are struggling financially.

- Review Chromebook care and digital citizenship rules with the student body.

- Purchase a program like GoGuardian to monitor Chromebook internet traffic and to prevent inappropriate searches.

- Conduct a Tech Night or Chromebook Overview Screencast so that parents understand the nuts and bolts of a learning environment that relies heavily on Chromebooks rather than books and lined paper.

- Know your students' financial situation. Wi-Fi may not be accessible at home and alternative options must be explored. For example, www.everyoneon.org connects families with substantially discounted internet plans for the home.

What YOU Can Do Tomorrow

CLASSROOM: Provide students with consistent access to Chromebooks. Just as we expect students to bring their books and binders home, we should expect them to bring their Chromebooks back and forth from home. Homework assignments should consist of students using their Chromebooks to write, read, and create.

SCHOOL: Provide staff with innovative Chromebook training opportunities. If we expect students to use

Chromebooks, then we must expect staff members to use Chromebooks. Particularly in a 1:1 learning environment, teaching staff must be given their own Chromebooks. They need to know how Chromebooks work so they can troubleshoot issues and use a common language with students. Districts must support staff with training and time to acclimate to their Chromebooks. Many districts are hiring technology coaches to help teachers thrive in their 1:1 environment. In addition, they are empowering their teachers to become Level 1 and 2 Certified Educators, Certified Trainers, and Innovators. Visit https://edutrainingcenter.withgoogle.com/training to learn more about self-paced training. Other districts are hiring consulting firms, like Evolving Educators LLC (www.evolvingeducators.com), who have Google Certified Trainers on staff to help with moving 1:1 Chromebook environments forward in a positive direction.

DISTRICT: Provide board of education members with access to Chromebooks. They can use their district-issued Chromebooks during meetings to access agendas and other pertinent documents. Board members can also bring their devices home for committee work purposes like receiving and reading emails. Districts must commit to posting agendas and other documents in Google Drive. Additionally, boards of education can streamline workflow and communication by using Google Classroom.

Chromebooks can benefit school districts by driving technology costs down, promoting cloud-based workflow, and providing an equal playing field for all stakeholders. Over time, Chromebooks will become a part of your school's culture and an important part of how students learn and create. Scan Image 17.1 to learn about the National Education Technology Plan and how you can ensure that technology is being used to promote the success of all students.

Image 17.1

HACK 18

MIRROR STUDENT AND STAFF ACHIEVEMENTS WITH CHROMECAST

THE PROBLEM: LEARNING ENVIRONMENTS LACK THE ABILITY TO CONNECT TO A MASS AUDIENCE

DO YOU REMEMBER when acknowledging student work or staff achievement was limited to a display on a bulletin board or an article in the local newspaper? What a feeling of pride that would bring to that particular person and the entire school community. There is no doubt that this sort of recognition still exists, but it can also be accomplished on a much larger scale. Over the past decade, technology has allowed people to mirror or wirelessly project from one device to another. Products like Apple TV, Mirroring360, and Google's Chromecast provide simple solutions to the dilemma of figuring out how to get what's on one computer screen to another screen.

> All sorts of student-created and student-centered content can be mirrored with Chromecast, including Google Slides, YouTube, or Chromebook screen.

A few years ago, a principal from Iowa tweeted out a simple picture of a monitor that was mounted in one of his school's hallways. There was nothing earth-shattering about the tweet itself, other than it told a story of how a television monitor could change the conversation about the awesome things taking place in a school. Brad was inspired by this concept and wanted to do the same thing at Black River Middle School in Chester, New Jersey. He reached out to the school's parent-teacher organization and pitched the idea of mounting a television in the front hallway to promote student and staff achievements and to inform stakeholders of school happenings. About a month later the dream became a reality. From that point forward students, staff, and parents enjoyed contributing to and seeing information, images, and initiatives displayed on the television monitor.

THE HACK: USE CHROMECAST TO MIRROR STUDENT AND STAFF ACHIEVEMENTS FROM ONE DEVICE TO ANOTHER

Chromecast is a small device that plugs into your television through the HDMI port. Once the device is plugged in, a series of steps needs to be taken to connect it to the internet. The easiest way to connect Chromecast to the internet is by downloading the Google Home app onto your Wi-Fi-enabled phone or through the Google Cast extension on your Chrome browser. Then you will open up the app or extension and follow the easy setup instructions. The Chromecast device speaks with the Google Home app or the Google Cast extension in the Chrome browser through the same Wi-Fi network.

Once the device has been configured you can begin streaming from your mobile device or laptop. For example, if you are on the YouTube app on your

phone or the YouTube website on your laptop, you will notice a little monitor icon to click. It will prompt you to cast the video to the Chromecast-enabled television monitor. Once you click the button, you will notice that the picture on your phone or laptop is now on the television monitor. It essentially mirrors what's on one device

Image 18.1

to another. Scan Image 18.1 to visit Google's site to learn more about how Chromecast works and what it looks like to access the Chromecast website.

What
YOU
Can Do Tomorrow

CLASSROOM: Project student work to a SMART Board or screen. Students love to share their individual or group work. All sorts of student-created and student-centered content can be mirrored with Chromecast including Google Slides, YouTube, or Chromebook screen. Students just need to download the Google Cast extension from the Chrome Store. Scan Image 18.2 to download the extension.

Image 18.2

Once it's downloaded, the icon will show up in the upper right-hand corner of the Chrome browser. If students wanted to present a Google Slide presentation to the entire class, they would open up their presentation, click the Google Cast icon, and select the teacher's Chromecast option. The students then get to assume the teacher role by walking classmates through the presentation.

SCHOOL: Jazz up your hallway, cafeteria, or heavily trafficked areas with a flat-panel television. Purchase a Chromecast device and connect to the flat-panel television. As the assistant principal at Black River Middle School, Brad pushes out content to the Chromecast-enabled television monitor. Brad displays a daily motivational quotation via Google Slides. Students and staff see the visual as they walk by, reading a quotation that may inspire them. On other days, students or teachers will send Brad digital content that they've created for a class project or to promote an upcoming extra-curricular event. A Student of the Day initiative could also take advantage of the Chromecast and flat-panel television monitor. Each day the big screen highlights a student from each grade level for all to see.

DISTRICT: Stream important documents, presentations, and videos to a television at district-level committee meet-ings or board of education meetings. Occasions arise at various points throughout the school year to present stan-dardized test results or curriculum projects to the public. Using a mirroring tool like Chromecast will assist in providing a clear and graphically appealing presentation for all to enjoy.

Chromecast pushes classroom, school, or district-related content out from your laptop or phone to a television with a few clicks of the mouse or taps of the screen. The device is a fairly inexpensive way to celebrate student and staff achievements and display important information for stakeholders. Take a risk and ask your school to purchase a Chromecast to try out in one of your classes, schools, or meetings. Engagement will increase, and a sense of pride will emerge that improves the overall culture in your learning environment.

CHANGE THE FACE OF FIELD TRIPS WITH GOOGLE CARDBOARD

THE PROBLEM: FIELD TRIPS ARE TOO EXPENSIVE

BACK IN THE Spring of 2013, Brad's school was lucky enough to pilot Google Cardboard. So many barriers prevent good, old-fashioned field trips from taking place that now most schools are looking for alternatives. Leading up to his school's pilot program, Brad was thinking about some of these obstacles and alternatives. Field trips have become incredibly expensive. Some of the places Brad would like to send his teachers are impossible to access due to geographic barriers or costs associated with the trip. He has noticed that teachers have relied on video clips, movies, magazines, and WebQuests to give their students a flavor of how places look and feel. We all know that there is no better thing than reality. Some lucky students are able to actually visit a famous place or landmark like Independence Hall in Philadelphia, or Ellis Island in New York by the time they graduate. However, sometimes the real deal just isn't possible when it comes to travel. Enter Google technology.

> **Host a virtual reality night for all stakeholders to actively experience this particularly innovative learning environment.**

Google Cardboard offers exciting new avenues to enhance student engagement with the world and promote active learning. Changing the culture of your classroom with a class set of Google Cardboard viewers can engage students in relevant learning experiences. As teachers, we always want to make sure that students learn in unique ways and get excited about the topic at hand.

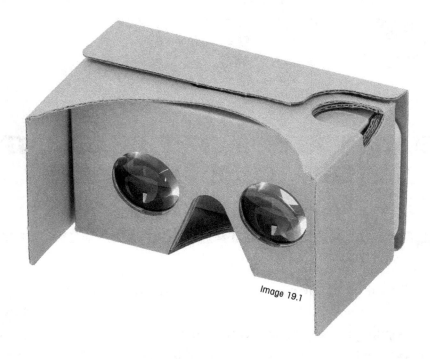

Image 19.1

THE HACK: TRANSFORM THE FIELD TRIP WITH GOOGLE CARDBOARD

Google Cardboard looks similar to an old-fashioned viewfinder as you can see in Image 19.1. For those not familiar, a viewfinder is an item people can hold up to their eyes to view different images or video. Google Cardboard transforms the old-fashioned viewfinder into a virtual reality experience. Once you purchase and download one of the many Cardboard apps from the Apple or Play Store, you can stick your cell phone into the Cardboard and go on a field trip anywhere in the world. Visit the solar system. Learn about daily life in ancient Egypt. It's all possible with Google Cardboard.

What **YOU** Can Do Tomorrow

CLASSROOM: Take your students on a virtual field trip.
Several apps facilitate virtual reality (VR) trips. Subject-specific VR apps like Egypt Chamber, which is free, will immerse students in the history of ancient civilizations. Another option, Expeditions, a paid VR app, enables teachers to lead the entire class through a virtual field trip and support student explorations of various places around the world. To use Expeditions, you will first need to download the app from the Play Store or Apple store. Next, slide your device into your viewer. Then, open the app and choose Guide mode to set up the expedition experience. Once in Guide mode, select the expedition that you want your class to explore. Then the student explorers can click the "follow" button on the screen that they see in their viewers.

SCHOOL: Secure funding for your staff. Support your staff by helping them find money for Cardboard through grants, school budget line items, or requests to the school's parent-teacher organization or education foundation. A simple Google Cardboard viewer costs around $15. An entire Google Expeditions Kit costs around $10,000, and includes a class set of devices, viewers, a router, case, and other items.

DISTRICT: Invite parents, board of education members, and the community at large to share in the Google Cardboard experience. Host a virtual reality night for all stakeholders to actively experience this particularly innovative learning environment. This sort of offering will garner support

> for future funding of virtual reality initiatives. It's also important to look at changing your district policy to allow students to use cellphones for a learning experience that integrates virtual reality.

One of our jobs as educators is to move students from on-task to engaged. Integrating a learning tool like Google Cardboard can get students excited about the topic at hand. It's important to start small and maybe purchase or have someone donate a simple viewer. Try it out at home with your family and then test it out with one of your classes. Then bring in some more viewers and make them a part of a learning station. Ultimately, your goal would be to have a whole class set. Virtual reality could be the missing piece to making learning come alive for students. Students will never forget the memories they had when using Google Cardboard in your class.

HACK 20

PERSONALIZE, EXPAND, AND SHARE WITH THE CHROME WEB STORE

THE PROBLEM: WHAT CAN THE CHROME WEB STORE DO FOR ME?

WHETHER YOU ARE new to using Google Apps for Education or an experienced Googler, using the Chrome Web Store can seem like a daunting task when you see lots of apps and have no idea where to begin. Many people overlook or underestimate what the Chrome Web Store can do for them and thus they don't look into its use, or simply go on it to download something and then close out the window. This online store provides free web applications that are easily downloadable with a single click for your Google Chrome browser. It is so much more than a site that just downloads apps: Every educator should give this feature a second look.

> **Harnessing features in the Chrome Web Store will help you personalize, manage, and share Google.**

Scott came across some great educational uses of the Chrome Web Store by accident. He was looking for an app to download and happened to see the gear on the top right of the page next to his email address. He clicked it, not knowing what it did, but by doing so he opened up the world of the Chrome Web Store. He now regularly uses it for himself and to share with others.

THE HACK: CUSTOMIZE, MANAGE, AND
SHARE IN THE CHROME WEB STORE

To find the web applications and extensions available on the Chrome Web Store, start by clicking the "Apps" button on the top left of your browser and then clicking the "Web Store" icon that comes up on your screen.

Google has designed the applications and extensions to customize your Google experience, manage what you have downloaded, and share that information with others. This site makes it easy to do each of these in a single click on your screen. Expand your experience and knowledge of Google by looking around the Chrome Store.

 **What**
YOU
Can Do Tomorrow

CLASSROOM: Customize your Google Chrome page with a theme from the Chrome Web Store. How cool would it be to have a customized Chrome page related to a new topic being studied in class when your students open up the browser on the Chromebooks or computers in your classroom? It's

Image 20.1

simple and adds a nice personal touch to your classroom and your students' learning experience. There are many free images to select from. You can quickly make the change to your browser: Go to the Chrome Web Store's themes page by scanning the QR code in Image 20.1 and

then select a theme that is displayed on the screen or by using the "search the store" space on the top left. Select a theme by clicking on the theme you want for your browser and downloading it.

When your students open their Chrome browsers, they will see the classroom or subject theme, making for a more personalized learning experience. Be careful, though: Your students will now be searching for the next theme for your classroom computers.

SCHOOL: **Manage the apps and extensions you have downloaded to Chrome in the Chrome Web Store.** Sometimes you find something you like in the Chrome Web Store and download it but forget about it. Or you think you have downloaded something but can't find it. Or you are trying to maintain continuity of apps among multiple devices in a school. It's easy to manage your apps and extensions by signing in to Chrome and going to the Chrome Web Store. The easiest way is to click on the nine-dot, multicolored box (the waffle) with the word "Apps" next to it on the top left of your browser page, which we have shown in Image 20.2. Click on the "Chrome Web Store" icon, and when it opens you will see your email address and a gear on the top right. Click the gear and then "Your Apps." You can now review your apps and click on them to review what they do.

Image 20.2 Google and the Google logo are registered trademarks of Google Inc., used with permission.

You can also search for similar apps on this page by clicking on the apps you have downloaded so the information screen about the app pops up. For a school trying to maintain continuity among its devices, this is an easy way to achieve that goal.

DISTRICT: **Push out a specific app or extension to others through email.** Building and district administrators should use this feature in the Chrome Web Store when they find a useful app or extension for themselves and other educators. First, sign in to Chrome and go to the Chrome Web Store. Remember to click on the waffle on the top left of your browser page (see Image 20.2). Click on the "Chrome Web Store" icon so you see your email address and a gear on the top right. Click the gear

ADD TO CHROME

Image 20.3 Google and the Google logo are registered trademarks of Google Inc., used with permission.

and then "Your Apps." Notice the symbol displayed in Image 20.3 to the right. Click on it.

You now have an option to email it to a person or group of people you think would be interested. Share it to help someone become better with Google. In Scott's district he has a Lead Learner Committee (LLC) that works on identifying educational technology. This feature is perfect for them to push out a great app they find to the rest of the district.

Some of the most underappreciated features in Google will make you a more effective and efficient educator. Harnessing features in the Chrome Web Store will help you personalize, manage, and share Google. Using the Chrome Web Store on a consistent basis will increase your use of apps that make you, students, and colleagues more productive.

HACK 21

EXPAND YOUR USE OF GOOGLE WITH EXTENSIONS

THE PROBLEM: HOW TO BECOME A MORE EFFECTIVE USER OF GOOGLE

G SUITE'S AMAZING ABILITY to help us as educators rests in its ability to share files and collaborate on the same Google app, whether it is Docs, Sheets, Slides, or another feature. Its unparalleled functions are often mimicked by other software providers. Once you understand and use the many features in the G Suite for Education, you will want to become a more effective user so you can manage your time more efficiently. To do this you can use Google extensions in collaboration with various G Suite resources.

In Hack 20 we explained how to personalize Chrome, download apps and extensions, and push them out to others. Now it's time to take that knowledge to the next level. In this chapter we highlight some extensions that will make you a more effective user of Google. Scott has found Google extensions that allow him to be more effective while teaching educators, responding to emails with common phrases or statements, and enhancing the social media presence of his school district. The extensions he

> This extension provides you with time-saving keyboard shortcuts that insert preset messages. You download the extension and set your messages up with the shortcuts.

uses improve Google's functionality, and allow him the ability to complete tasks more efficiently so he can work on other things.

THE HACK: USE SPECIFIC GOOGLE EXTENSIONS TO BECOME A MORE EFFECTIVE GOOGLER

A Google Extension software program has a specific function which can modify or enhance one or more G Suite programs. Download extensions from the Chrome Store onto your Chrome browser. You will see its symbol on your Chrome browser when you open it. They are easy to use, serve a specific purpose, and make you a more effective Googler. The Chrome Web Store has hundreds, if not thousands, of extensions available for download. You only need to search the store, find what you are looking for, and download it. Check out Hack 20 for more information on how to search for, download, and manage your extensions.

 **What YOU Can Do Tomorrow**

CLASSROOM: Stop worrying about the commercial that will play when you show a YouTube video in class. We all love to enhance our lessons through videos. Films can make connections to content being taught and provide excellent visual and auditory experiences. Many of those videos come from YouTube. We appreciate and respect the free access this site provides and have no issue with commercials playing prior to viewing videos. However, when these videos are used in the classroom environment and the teacher has no control over the content of the commercial, we need something to help us control the learning environment. We like Adblock for YouTube. See image 21.1 for what the extension looks like.

Once you download Adblock to your Chrome browser, no commercial will pop up before you show your video. You can take a deep breath and press play without worrying about unexpected, and possibly inappropriate content.

Adblock for Youtube™
Productivity

image 21.1 Google and the Google logo are registered trademarks of Google Inc., used with permission.

SCHOOL: Preset auto responses to common statements and comments you make in emails. We often receive emails that require the same response or comment. It might be a simple, "Thank You" or "I've received your email." Other times it's a response to dozens of emails with the same comment. Typing these responses can be time-consuming and a poor use of time. We like to use Auto Text Expander from the Chrome Store.

Auto Text Expander for ...
Productivity

image 21.2 Google and the Google logo are registered trademarks of Google Inc., used with permission.

This extension provides you with time-saving keyboard shortcuts that insert preset messages. You download the extension and set your messages up with the shortcuts. Do remember that it's case sensitive. Here are two of Scott's favorites:

Typing "Thx" produces "Thanks for the email. I will be in contact soon."

Typing his secretary's initials produces "Please contact my secretary for an appointment."

These preset auto responses make you a more effective educator and communicator, and, let's be honest, it's a cool feature.

DISTRICT: **Use customized images to communicate with your school district and community.** It's our responsibility to provide our school district and community with information about all the great things happening in our district. We can do that the traditional way by sending a message. However, social media now offers more engaging ways to do this through images and customized pictures. You can create your own images quickly and effectively through Chrome extensions like Awesome Screenshot Capture and Annotate.

image 21.3 Google and the Google logo are registered trademarks of Google Inc., used with permission.

Scott uses this extension multiple times a week to create images to send out to his school district and community through the district's social media feeds. Two important notes: (I) ensure that you have the rights to use the image you take from the web (check out Hack I5 for more details on this issue); (2) be sure you have permission from parents to post students' faces. This should be accomplished yearly through an acceptable use form in your school district.

Once you download the Awesome Screenshot Capture and Annotate extension, you will see its symbol, a camera lens, on your Chrome browser. Find the image you want to use online or use a picture you have taken and click on the camera lens symbol. It will offer you a series of choices to grab the image. Scott always uses the "Capture Selected Area" because he can crop the image. Once you select the area you want to use, that image will open in another Chrome window where you can crop the image, put a shape in or around it, insert an arrow, straight line, or free-formed line, highlight an area, write text, or blur something.

After editing the image, click the "Done" button and the extension asks you where you want the image. You may save the image as a file, copy it to your clipboard, or print the screenshot—your choice is final, so choose wisely. Scott usually chooses one of the first two. If he wants to use the file multiple times, he will save it as a file on his desktop or in Google Drive. If he wants to use it once only by pasting it into a Doc, he will copy it to his clipboard, go to where he wants it, and paste it by right-clicking his mouse.

We use the G Suite because we appreciate its many features that make us more effective, efficient educators. Google extensions expands the functionality of Google even further. Don't stop with the three options we've outlined here. Check out our chapter on the Google Chrome Store for more information on how to find and use other extensions and become a better Googler.

HACK 22

FLIP FACULTY MEETINGS AND LEARNING SPACES WITH SCREENCASTIFY

THE PROBLEM: STUDENTS AND TEACHERS DO NOT HAVE TIME FOR IMMERSION

HAVE YOU EVER asked teachers or administrators about their thoughts on faculty meetings? Most teachers despise sitting in a room every month, hearing agenda item after agenda item read aloud so that "everyone has gotten the message." Most administrators stress over the fact that they feel required to plan and run these traditional gatherings. Just for a few seconds, imagine a faculty meeting where you have an opportunity to share best practices, discuss emerging trends, analyze current research, or collaborate on a unit of study. Sounds pretty good, right? Fortunately, we are seeing pockets of this sort of "immersion mindset" in schools around the world, where teachers have autonomy to take control of their professional growth during faculty meeting time.

While teachers' time is being wasted during faculty meetings, consider the use of student time in the classroom. Accountability measures and prescribed curricula may limit what can be done. As a result, students' "on-task" time often centers around a scripted lesson plan. The teacher might feel compelled to control every single

> **People appreciate it when others respect their time.**

portion of the lesson, and therefore cannot engage students to the extent that might be possible. Students need time in class to collaborate with peers and be supported by teachers. Flipping teacher-directed activities, such as the lecture, can free up time for students to engage in meaningful learning experiences. Google offers the potential for this type of learning environment to exist.

THE HACK: CREATE SCREENCASTS WITH THE SCREENCASTIFY GOOGLE CHROME EXTENSION

Maximize time by flipping the environment you are in charge of creating. This will help free up time for students in class and administrators and teachers in faculty meetings so everyone can participate in engaging learning experiences. Use the Screencastify Google Chrome extension to capture what's on your computer screen through a recorded video. Visit the Chrome Web Store and type in the word Screencastify to select and download the extension.

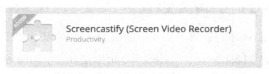

Image 22.1 Google and the Google logo are registered trademarks of Google Inc., used with permission.

Take a look at Image 22.1 for what the extension looks like in the Chrome Web Store.

For clarification purposes, an extension extends or enhances the functionality of the Chrome browser. So in this case, the Screencastify extension tells the Chrome browser that it's okay to record the screen. Once the extension is downloaded, you will notice the corresponding icon in the upper right-hand corner of your screen. When you're ready, click the "Screencastify" icon and follow the prompts to successfully capture an image or record a screencast.

What
YOU
Can Do Tomorrow

CLASSROOM: Transform your lecture by creating a brief 10-minute interactive screencast for your lesson or homework. This option serves students better than a 45-minute lecture. You will start to notice that you can say a lot more in less time with a screencast. Students can use the class time that is freed up to collaborate on projects and explore topics that matter to them; your time will be well spent supporting students in more productive ways. Better yet, have your students create their own screencasts to teach themselves and others about the topic at hand. Students could show others how to solve math equations or provide insight on a scientific concept like the periodic table of elements.

SCHOOL: Flip your faculty meeting agenda by recording a 5-minute screencast. This is much easier to digest than being talked at for 45 minutes during a traditional faculty meeting. Your recording can be blasted out to staff via email a day prior to the meeting. A large chunk of time is now freed up for meaningful learning and collaboration on topics that affect the success of all students. Teachers could explore educational apps or websites, participate in a book talk, or discuss research methods that help address issues they are experiencing.

DISTRICT: Communicate with stakeholders using the Screencastify extension. Sometimes community members cannot attend important district-wide meetings pertaining to standardized testing or online safety. Simply open the Google

Slide deck or other resources you shared during the actual presentation. Then, activate the Screencastify extension and begin recording your screencast. Once complete, upload it to Google Drive and share out the link to stakeholders for them to view at their own leisure.

People appreciate it when others respect their time. Minimizing mundane lecture time with students in the classroom or teachers in a faculty meeting can boost morale and provide folks with an opportunity to dive deep into topics that genuinely interest them. Screencastify is just one of many ways to flip typical learning experiences.

HACK 23

BUILD YOUR LEARNING
COMMUNITY WITH GOOGLE+

THE PROBLEM: EDUCATORS FEEL DISCONNECTED
FROM THE REST OF THE WORLD

EDUCATORS OFTEN FEEL like they're working in their own little bubbles without an authentic space to share, connect, learn, reflect, and collaborate. If you do not agree with this, take a few moments and think about these questions:

- How long have you or another educator kept ideas and tricks to yourself within the confines of your own classroom or office?

- When is the last time you shared a lesson plan or idea with a colleague in your building or with a complete educational stranger halfway across the globe?

- How difficult is it for you to find relevant resources that push your thinking?

- Why is it important to stay connected as an educator?

> As resources and ideas emerge, post them to your PLC's Google+ Community. This sort of hybrid PLC model streamlines the process of sharing and interacting.

Every educator has something of worth to share. It could be a lesson plan, teaching strategy, technology integration tip, or a way to reach struggling students. Technology presents educators with opportunities to connect and share in novel ways. With a few clicks of the mouse or taps of the screen you can evolve as an educator and ultimately impact student success. Often, though, educators feel reluctant to expand their personal learning networks due to lack of administrative support, time constraints, or because they simply don't know what they don't know. Given an opportunity to sharpen their skills in the virtual world with a tool like Google+, educators will rise to the occasion and drive change.

THE HACK: EXPAND YOUR PERSONAL LEARNING NETWORK

Take advantage of Google+ to expand your personal learning network. Google+ is a social media program that connects you with other professionals in the same fashion as Twitter, Facebook, or LinkedIn. It's linked to your Google account, so you can connect and share using other Google products.

Image 23.1 Google and the Google logo are registered trademarks of Google Inc., used with permission.

Access Google+ by locating and clicking on it through the waffle, or you can do a Google search for Google+. As long as you are logged in to your Google account it will bring you to where you need to go.

Take a few moments and look around at all of the different features Google+ has to offer. You will notice the stream front and center. This is where you can post and see content, similar to other social media services. Take a look at Image 23.1 to see the various options users have when posting content.

Images, links, polls, text, and location can be pushed out to your PLN on Google+. The three little dots, or what we like to call the traffic signal, allow users to disable re-sharing or having others comment on the post.

Once you are ready to publish content, click the blue "Post" button. You will notice the post is now in your stream on the Google+ homepage. Locate the "Collections" tab on the left-hand side of your Google+ page. This feature allows you to categorize posts by topic. Scan the QR code in Image 23.2 and follow the Hacking Google for

Image 23.2

Education Google+ Collections page to stay on top of best practices related to all things G Suite for Education.

Communities, another feature of Google+, works along similar lines as Collections, providing users with the ability to post and start conversations around various topics. However, Collections is simple and topic-specific, whereas Communities is more wide open.

We wanted to create a place for fans of Hacking Google for Education to connect and share with one another, so we went onto Google+, clicked the "Communities" tab, clicked the "Yours" tab, clicked "Create a Community," named our Community, and made it public for all to follow. We now have a place to meet and share the great Google resources out there for educators.

If you need to access and change your profile, simply click on the "Profile" tab on the left-hand side of the page. Click the "Edit Profile" button to customize your page. The "People" feature gives you a chance to find people, access your followers, and see who is following you. You can also use the "Event" feature to invite people in your Google networks to your virtual or physical events.

What **YOU** Can Do Tomorrow

CLASSROOM: Create a virtual classroom community that provides support services to address the needs of all learners. Use the Google+ Collections feature to post content for your students as they navigate their way through a particular unit of study. For example, imagine a world language class where students can access content related to the culture of a French- or Spanish-speaking country. Once the teacher posts content, students can access it through their Google+ accounts and comment with additional resources that they found useful. To take things a step further, students could create their own collections on a topic they are currently learning about. It could be vetted and used by peers as well as students from around the world.

SCHOOL: Participate in a virtual professional learning community with subject-area or grade-level colleagues. Using the Community feature in Google+, you can share and comment on colleagues' resources. For example, literacy teachers could form a PLC to focus on nonfiction

Image 23.3 Google and the Google logo are registered trademarks of Google Inc., used with permission.

reading strategies. As resources and ideas emerge, post them to your PLC's Google+ Community. This sort of hybrid PLC model streamlines the process of sharing and interacting. You do not even have to meet in the physical world since much of the work can be accomplished virtually. See Image 23.3 for the Communities button.

DISTRICT: Communicate information and share resources with a district-wide committee. Every district can benefit from using a Google+ community to organize its numerous district-wide committees. For example, your district might focus on a 1:1 Chromebook learning environment. This sort of initiative is a huge undertaking that affects all stakeholders. It's important to form a committee that includes parents, students, community members, and educators to ensure the initiative ultimately rolls out with success. Over the course of the planning period and eventual rollout, members can share ideas and resources to steer the committee vision. Agendas, meeting minutes, and subcommittee work can be shared out within the Google+ community as well.

Google+ is a very useful collaboration and communication tool for all stakeholders. It can facilitate change, enhance your effectiveness, and connect you with other game-changers in the educational world. Google+ can help you bridge the divide between the physical and virtual worlds. It provides users with an opportunity to amplify their voices and come out of isolation.

HACK 24

STREAM YOUTUBE TO DRIVE CHANGE

THE PROBLEM: INTEGRATING VIDEO INTO THE CLASSROOM TAKES TIME

IN 2005, A social studies teacher would have to sign out a laptop/LCD projector cart from the school library and roll it down to his classroom. He'd then reach down to the bottom of the cart, take out the fifty-foot ethernet wire, plug it into the laptop, run it through to the back of the classroom, and plug into the ethernet jack. The teacher would turn on the computer, open up the internet browser, and access a streaming video service. He'd conduct a search to locate a geography video on Latin America. After he finally located a twenty-minute video clip, he'd have to begin the download process. Approximately forty-five minutes later the video would be ready to play for his students. Fast forward to the present: People of all ages have almost instant access to television shows, videos, and movies on their devices. Students can open up their school-issued Chromebooks, quickly browse the internet, and begin streaming a video without even blinking. Teachers can quickly find streaming educational content and play it or share out to the class with a tool like Google Classroom.

The issue that comes with this territory is that educators need time and support to learn how to integrate streaming content into their settings. Not only do students have access to all kinds of content, but they can now create their own and share it with the world. Schools

> **You will want to explore all that YouTube has to offer.**

are now confronted with the dilemma of how much freedom they give to students and staff when it comes to web streaming services like YouTube. Technology is a double-edged sword. There are so many wonderful things that you can do with it to make life better, while poor choices can create a negative situation.

Although our first impulse may be to dwell on what could go wrong with a tool like YouTube, the positives outweigh the negatives. Embracing the possibilities of YouTube can drive change and give a voice to all stakeholders.

THE HACK: STREAM VIDEOS
WITH A PUSH OF A BUTTON

Believe it or not, YouTube was bought by Google way back in 2006. So technically, YouTube is a Google product. Sign in to YouTube with your Google account using the waffle. See Image 24.1 for the location. You may also conduct a Google search to find YouTube.

Image 24.1 Google and the Google logo are registered trademarks of Google Inc., used with permission.

You will want to explore all that YouTube has to offer. Feel free to download the YouTube app to your Apple or Android phone and explore that way as well. You will notice the "Home" tab in the upper left-hand corner of the screen. The videos you have watched and your recommendations will pop up here. The next tab down, "My Channel," is where you will build a channel for your classroom, school, or district initiative. It's essentially the profile page where you can add a profile picture, background, and other important information about your channel. Some of the parts of your channel page that you want to pay attention to are the Uploads, Playlists, Liked Videos, and Subscriptions.

You will notice an arrow pointing upwards in the upper right-hand corner, denoting the place where you can upload a video to your channel. Select the video that you want uploaded from your device and begin the upload process. You can set the video upload to public, unlisted, or private. Completed uploads appear in your feed. While you're in the "My Channel" part of YouTube, explore the "Video Manager" feature that is located at the top of the page.

Here you can edit your uploaded videos, change view settings, and see analytics. You can also create a playlist of videos specific to a particular topic. The "Playlist" will be part of your channel and can be set to public or private. Take a few moments right now to create your channel, upload a video, and subscribe to other channels that interest you. The "Subscription" tab allows users to subscribe to channels. For example, if you are looking for math videos, the Khan Academy Channel might be worth subscribing to. Make sure to click the red "Subscribe" button to stay current with videos that are added to the channel.

What YOU Can Do Tomorrow

CLASSROOM: Ask students to curate a video tutorial playlist related to the concepts they are studying. Say, for example, students need additional supporting content to make sense of algebra problems they are learning about in class. Give them class time to browse through online videos and add them to a playlist they have created on YouTube. They can now use these tutorials to support their learning. Take learning a step further and have students create screencasts of themselves solving algebraic problems and upload them to YouTube. Sometimes students learn best from other students.

SCHOOL: Conduct morning announcements on YouTube and stream them out to classrooms and the community. Have your Student Council produce and broadcast the morning announcement on your school's YouTube channel. All you need is a laptop or tripod/tablet setup to record your session.

Another option would be to try YouTube Live and send the archive of the recording to the Student Council channel. YouTube Live is a fairly new feature that replaced Google Hangouts On Air. Access YouTube Live by clicking on your profile picture in the upper right-hand corner of the YouTube screen. Select "Creator Studio" and click on "Live Streaming." A multistep process must be followed to activate the program. Have students take ownership of their school culture.

DISTRICT: Maintain a district-wide YouTube channel to broadcast events, concerts, professional development programs, guest speakers, and so much more. People lead busy lives and may not be able to attend the hundreds of school and district functions throughout the school year. Streaming video comes to the rescue. For example, you might have one of your local police officers speak to your parents about online safety. Parents who cannot be present at 9:30 in the morning can watch on the district YouTube channel.

YouTube can engage students in their learning and connect with stakeholders. Rather than trying to YouTube everything right off the bat, start small, maybe with having one class create a tutorial channel or record one event just so you can get your feet wet. As time goes on and you get more used to the process, expand your YouTube offerings. Make sure to enlist the help of students to assist with production and archiving.

CONNECT YOUR DISTRICT WITH HANGOUTS

THE PROBLEM: OUR INTERACTIONS ARE LIMITED BY LOCATION AND COST

BRINGING IN VIRTUAL guest speakers is a wonderful way to supplement lessons and expose students to all kinds of new people. Brad was thinking about exactly these kinds of roadblocks when a Spanish teacher approached him to discuss ways to enhance students' knowledge of the culture of Spain. Taking a field trip was not logistically possible. But an idea had occurred to the teacher: They could conduct a Google Hangout with a family from Spain that was vacationing in the United States.

A student in the class was close friends with the family, and they agreed to do a Google Hangout with the Spanish class. Brad stopped by to see firsthand how the teacher empowered the student to conduct and share the Google Hangout on a mobile device. Students were able to interact and ask questions with the family from Spain and gain valuable perspective on the language and culture.

> Break down the walls of classrooms, buildings, and school districts with Hangouts.

We want the ability to give our students an experience that extends beyond our four walls of the classroom. When students are able to engage with other students from classrooms in different parts of the United States or the world, they grow exponentially. The benefits of connecting through Hangouts can extend to entire schools and districts as well.

THE HACK: USE GOOGLE HANGOUTS TO ENHANCE YOUR SCHOOL COMMUNITY

Hangouts can work for any level classroom, any size school building, or any district. Hangouts allows for video conferences with up to fifteen connected computers at one time. Your district IT does need to verify Hangouts and turn it on, and you will also need a computer that has access to a video camera, a projector, and sound to get the most out of your hangout. While numerous webcams can be used to hook

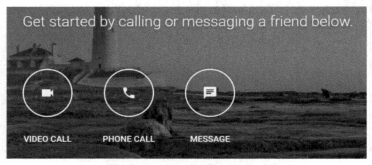

Image 25.1 Google and the Google logo are registered trademarks of Google Inc., used with permission.

up to a camera, Billy has found the best type can be hooked up to a tripod so that you can move it around if need be. You can access Hangouts in your waffle. Once you have clicked on it you will get a screen that asks you if you want to call or message a friend. See Image 25.1 for the choices that will show up.

Image 25.2 Google and the Google logo are registered trademarks of Google Inc., used with permission.

When you select one, for example, "video call," you will be asked to invite people. Start typing friends' names or emails and then click "invite." Your friends will receive a notice so they can accept the Hangout. Image 25.2 shows the screen where you can invite friends to your Hangout.

What YOU Can Do Tomorrow

CLASSROOM: Connect with the classroom next to your room. This is a simple way to test out Google Hangouts to make sure it works. Have a quick interaction with another classroom or share a story that you are reading in class. Once you are comfortable with using Google Hangouts, invite your colleague's class to participate in a competition or another more involved interaction. Then branch out to other educators in your Professional Learning Network who are willing to connect with you and do Hangouts with your class.

SCHOOL: Bring in a guest speaker. The costs of travel and other fees make bringing in a guest speaker prohibitive. Google Hangouts can allow you to bring in those same speakers at a discounted rate or even for free in some cases, depending on the speaker. There are so many different occasions where this could come in handy, including assemblies on bullying, famous authors, Read Across America week, and Hour of Code week.

DISTRICT: Organize PLCs across multiple buildings. Some districts have numerous buildings. Teachers who teach the same grade level may be in different buildings and so rarely talk with each other. Connect your schools to those in other school districts or communities to extend learning. One example of this might be when a district wants to bring in a consultant, but the consultant can only be in one building at a time. A district can use Google Hangouts to connect all of the buildings at one time to meet with the consultant.

Break down the walls of classrooms, buildings, and school districts with Hangouts. It allows communication to occur in real time so ideas get shared beyond our walls. Not only do students gain valuable experiences by talking with other classrooms virtually, but staff members can enhance their learning in a cost-effective way.

HACK 26

TRAVEL THE WORLD WITH GOOGLE MAPS

THE PROBLEM: STUDENTS NEED LOCAL, STATE, NATIONAL, AND GLOBAL AWARENESS

A s a former social studies teacher, Scott worked on helping his students understand the regions of the world, different cultures, and to identify specific locations relative to his school. He taught using books, maps hanging on the wall, and the ever-present classroom globe. But he realized these tools did not always give the students the context and perspective for them to fully understand how vast and geographically varied the world is.

THE HACK: USE GOOGLE MAPS TO TEACH GEOGRAPHY AND GLOBAL AWARENESS

Google Maps provides us both a detailed local and global perspective of the world from the comfort of our classrooms or homes. You can access Google Maps in your list of Google Apps via computer or laptop. You can also download the app onto your phone from the Chrome Web Store. Once you have accessed Google Maps you can find local or global places by using the "Search

> During Scott's first superintendent position, he used a combination of Google Maps and social media to keep the community engaged during the summer months.

139

Google Maps" option on the top left of the page. You now have access to maps of every location around the world at your hands.

The simplest way to start using Google Maps is to open the app on your computer or phone and type a location into the "Search Google Maps." Scan the QR code in Image 26.1 to get started.

Image 26.1

If, for instance, you type "Yankee Stadium," you will get a map on the right and information on the left. The information on the left is referred to as the side panel; it gives you details and pictures of the location you selected. Take a look at the pictures Google provides. At the time of this book's printing, there were 198 photos of the stadium available, along with the stadium address and phone number. The map on the right looks like a map rather than a satellite view. You can get the satellite view by clicking the three small boxes at the bottom right of the screen. As you scroll over them it will say "Show imagery." Refer to Image 26.2 for a look at this section of Google Maps.

Click "Show imagery" to see the options. Select the "Earth" option. Voila! You now have the satellite view of Yankee Stadium. Doesn't it look awesome? You can now move the image by putting your cursor on the image and dragging in whatever direction you want to move it. You can also zoom in or out on the map with the "+" and "-" symbols on the bottom right side of the map. Finally, you can rotate the view of the map with the red and white symbol on the bottom right.

What
YOU
Can Do Tomorrow

CLASSROOM: Focus locally or globally when you teach geography from Google Maps. At the start of each school year Scott used to quiz his high school freshmen to see their understanding of basic geography, like "What ocean would you swim in at the Jersey Shore?" and "Name a country in Europe." Afterwards, he'd go to the old, rolled-up map hanging in front of the chalkboard to go over the answers. Today, with Google Maps, we can make geography interactive and engaging for students.

SCHOOL: Develop community awareness of the areas around your school through Google Maps. It's important for schools to understand the communities that surround them. Google Maps makes it easier for the school community to understand and embrace their surrounding community. Once you have a general idea of how to search for a specific location, enter the street address of your school. A map of the school and surrounding area will come up, just as it did for our search of Yankee Stadium.

Image 26.2 Google and the Google logo are registered trademarks of Google Inc., used with permission.

See what's in your community by going back to the three little boxes on the bottom right of the screen, as seen in Image 26.2. Press the area of those boxes, which is the "Show imagery" section, and you will see a series of locations around your school at the bottom of your map. Scroll over one of those images: Google Maps will draw a line from the image at the bottom of the page to the actual location on the map. Now students can get a perspective of where the post office, town hall, or their favorite pizza place is located in respect to the school.

The "Browse street view images" option gives students more perspective of the community. Go back to the options at the bottom right of the page and you will see the shape of a person in yellow. Click on that person and drag it to a location. You will get a street-level view of the area. You can rotate this image by dragging on the image and moving it left, right, back, and forward. You can also "drive down the street" by moving your cursor over the image and clicking on the white arrow that pops up on the map. You can now take a virtual field trip right from the classroom.

DISTRICT: Create a fun and exciting experience for your school community over the summer using Google Maps. During Scott's first superintendent position, he used a combination of Google Maps and social media to keep the community engaged during the summer months. He created the hashtag #ChargersOnTheRoad and asked the community to take pictures of themselves in spirit wear that had the town name or the school mascot during vacations and college tours. He posted pictures or tweets with the hashtag on a Google Map for all to see, pinning the locations with the pictures. Here's how you can do this: Sign in to your Google account and go to "Google My Maps" by scanning the QR code in Image 26.3.

Image 26.3

Click "Create a New Map," which is in red on the top left. Add a title to the map in the "Untitled map" section on the top left. When you click to add a title, you can also add a description to explain to people what this map is all about. Click "save" when you are done. Use the search bar on the top to select an address or location. This is great for a district to promote the colleges or universities where students have been accepted. Once you have a college or university, choose one of the options on the map to add an image or video. Click on it. Now you can select an image from your files to add. You can also edit the information box or add additional information by clicking on the pencil image at the bottom of the box. Finally, customize the pin's color by clicking on the paint can at the bottom right and changing the icon for the pin.

You can make this a fun activity for the entire school district by creating a map and adding pictures of your students, staff, and community. It's also exciting to see how many places they go in the summer, making for a great opening conversation the next school year.

Google Maps can teach geography, encourage global awareness, and initiate community involvement. Create your own maps and pin locations with customized pictures for those pinned areas to engage your students and community. Have fun with Google Maps by creating exciting ways to use your maps as a classroom, school, and district.

HACK 27

ENHANCE GLOBAL LITERACY
WITH TOUR BUILDER

THE PROBLEM: LEARNING GLOBAL
LITERACY IS A CHALLENGE

GLOBAL LITERACY WAS once a tough issue to tackle—it was difficult for teachers to create learning experiences for their students that provided engaging insight on another part of the world. Textbooks, sharing pictures from a vacation, and magazine articles could only do so much. Solid understanding of the world is essential in our global society. Advances in technology, specifically with applications like Google Maps, Google Earth, and Tour Builder, provide the ability to create interactive visual representations that others can access easily.

Global literacy is a characteristic of a well-rounded education, and with that comes a belief that our individual experiences offer us varied perspectives of the world. Today's technology now enables people to see the world not only from their own perspectives, but from the perspectives of others.

> **People of all ages enjoy a great interactive story.**

THE HACK: MAKE GOOGLE EARTH INTERACTIVE

Google Tour Builder, an extension of Google Earth, allows users to create interactive and embedded geographical online experiences. Think of this program as an online tour of places you have visited on vacation or want people to know about. To activate Tour Builder, make sure you are logged into your Google account. Then, using the Chrome browser, type in the words "Google Tour Builder" and click on the first result. This will take you to the main page of the program. Browse through the information to become acclimated to how it works. A good starting point would be to click on the "View Tour" button or one of the "Featured Tours." Either option will give you a pretty good idea of what Tour Builder is all about.

Now it's time to create your own tour. To keep things simple, we will focus on your own life. Let's create a tour of places you have visited in the United States. The first thing you need to do is click on the "Create a Tour" button toward the top of the screen. Next you will give the tour a name, an author, and click the "Create Tour" button. This will bring you to a page where the tour can be built. The first part of the tour is the introduction. For our example you can type in information about various vacations that you have taken over the years. In this area you can add a photo that is symbolic of a vacation you have taken.

Then you will start to actually add locations to your tour. For example, say you once visited Lambertville, New Jersey. Click the "Add Location" button on the left-hand side of the page and type in the search box "Lambertville, New Jersey." The program will mark the map with a red place mark and a letter. Lambertville, New Jersey, should be marked with a letter A. You can then add information about the places you visited, the dates of the visits, and other important pieces of information. You will continue this process until all of the places you want on the tour are embedded on the interactive 3D map.

Tour Builder has some cool features for personalizing and editing. Click on the location that needs to be modified by locating the eye or the garbage can. It's also possible to change the placeholder icon to a different color or symbol by clicking on the "Change Icon" link toward the bottom. When you are done editing, you can share it with others by clicking the button in the right corner titled "Share." To access the tour you just created, click on the scroll-down arrow next to the home button and select "My Tours."

Need to go back and edit a tour you created? Click on the three lines, or what we like to call the hamburger, in the upper right-hand side of the screen. There are several options available, one of which allows you to edit a previously created tour. Other options include playing the tour in full screen and exporting it, or making a copy. Scan the QR code in Image 27.1 to see a Tour Builder exemplar.

Image 27.1

What
YOU
Can Do Tomorrow

CLASSROOM: Have students create an interactive online tour of a topic they are studying in social studies or a book they're reading in language arts class. Providing choice for students to show what they know about the topic at hand is really important. You could give the students the option to create a tour on Tour Builder about a historical location, the history of an event, or a favorite place they went on vacation.

SCHOOL: Conduct an online scavenger hunt activity for staff as a "getting to know you" activity for the first day of school or a faculty meeting. Prior to your first staff meeting, especially if you are a new administrator in the school, have folks take an online tour of your life so that they can get to know you. This approach accomplishes two things: Staff gets to know your background and you model the appropriate use of technology to engage learners. This activity could spill over to a discussion about how Tour Builder might be integrated into an upcoming lesson or unit of study.

> **DISTRICT:** Create a tour to highlight schools throughout your district. This will be a great opportunity to show off your school district to families that might be interested in moving into your community. Specific information about educational programs and extracurricular activities can be embedded.

Tour Builder allows classrooms, schools, and districts to tell their story and connect with people. People of all ages enjoy a great interactive story. Think about how Tour Builder might benefit your unique environment. Go ahead and open up Tour Builder and build a very simple tour just so you can get a feel for how it works, then share it with a few people and get some feedback. You will be amazed at how much others enjoy the stories you tell and even more amazed at what you can learn about others through the tours they build.

SHOW AND TELL WITH GOOGLE SITES

THE PROBLEM: BUILDING A WEBSITE IS CLUNKY AND DIFFICULT

ADMIT IT: AT some point in your educational career you were required to build and maintain a website. If not, it's probably going to happen in the very near future. The program that would assist you in this process was probably clumsy and difficult to navigate. Frequent calls to a tech-savvy colleague or the technology help-desk were probably commonplace. Once your classroom, school, or district website was built, it was probably just as clunky as the program itself. All you ever wanted was for a website design program to be user-friendly and not require a hundred-page manual.

> **Think about how you access information in today's world. You probably "Google it" right?**

Given that we live in a tech-driven society, students, teachers, and administrators must have the skill set to build some sort of website to convey messages and tell their story. Quite frankly, having a digital presence is no longer an option. Stakeholders now expect that a classroom, school, or district has a website with updated information.

THE HACK: SHOW AND TELL WITH SIMPLE WEBSITE DEVELOPMENT

Build a robust yet simple website with the Google Sites program. It's easy to use and is integrated with all of Google's tools of the trade, including Drive,

Maps, and YouTube. Open up the Chrome browser. Then, click on the waffle in the upper right-hand corner of the screen. Next, you will click on the "Sites" icon, which will lead you to the introductory page. From here you will click on the red "Create" button and select the option "in new sites." Now you are ready to create your very own website.

One of the first tasks you want to take care of when building a website in Google Sites is to give it a title. You can see in Image 28.1 that we gave our website the title Hacking Google for Education.

Image 28.1 Google and the Google logo are registered trademarks of Google Inc., used with permission.

When naming your own site, feel free to click inside the "Your Page Title Area" or on the actual site title in the upper left-hand corner to give the site a name. The next task is to decide what theme you would like to use—you have five options to choose from. Once the theme is selected you can edit the colors, font, and images to fit your personal preference.

Typically, the first page you create will be your homepage or what is called a landing page. In order to add additional webpages to your site, just click on the "Pages" tab on the right-hand side of screen. When you click the "Add Page" icon a new page will appear. At this point you can hover over the header and change the style to banner, larger banner, or title only, depending on how you want the actual webpage to look. Some people prefer one size header over another depending on whether an image or text is involved.

The "Insert" tab will assist you with building pages in your website. For example, you can insert YouTube videos, Google Drive folders, Calendars, Maps, and Google Forms. Say you wanted to embed a map on one of your webpages. Click the "Insert" tab, then click "Map." Using the search box, type in the location that you want to be featured on your webpage. Click the blue "Select" button to embed the map.

A number of editing features for new sections, such as the Map, will enhance the look and feel of your webpage. You can delete something you have embedded by clicking on the object and selecting the garbage can. Don't worry: If you accidentally delete a section you can click the "undo" button at the top of the page. You can change the section background color by hovering to the left of the section. From here you will notice a palette appear that contains various style options. The process repeats itself for any item that you want to embed on your webpage. The best thing you can do is create a sample website and begin to play around with the various features.

Here are four pointers that will support you in creating a simple yet powerful website:

1. Click the eye at the top of the screen to preview your website. There are three preview options: phone, tablet, large screen.

2. Add editors to help with building your website by clicking on the "Share" button next to the eye at the top of the screen.

3. Publish it for the world to see. Decide on what to call your website, type the name into the address box, and click "Publish."

4. Click the three little dots that we call the traffic light in the upper right-hand corner of the screen to access features like analytics and help.

What YOU Can Do Tomorrow

CLASSROOM: Design a unit of study that allows students to create a Google Site to show what they know. For example, college and career readiness is an important topic that students need to learn about, so work with your school librarian to develop a unit that has students research an occupation or college. As a culminating project, students can use Google Sites to design a website that highlights their research. The websites can be shared with family members, friends, and peers. Want to take things a step further? Allow students to interview someone associated with the research and embed the video onto the website.

SCHOOL: Curate a school-wide Google Site that houses best practice resources and provides teachers with a way to grow professionally. Educators are always looking for an easy way to access exceptional content that can enhance their effectiveness. Consider having building-level administrators or instructional coaches construct a website that features blog posts, video clips, and other educational material. These resources can be used in PLCs, at faculty meetings, or during a professional development day. Encourage staff members to contribute their own ideas and resources by filling out a Google Form. These resources will then be collected on an accompanying Google Sheet and can be added to the website.

DISTRICT: Redesign your district website using Google Sites to highlight student and staff achievements and inform stakeholders of district happenings. If you don't tell your district's story in the digital world, somebody else will, and it might be inaccurate. Establish a district-wide website committee to build a simple yet elegant website that engages and informs stakeholders. Over the next few months assign a handful of people to build the website at the classroom, school, district, and community levels. Once the site is complete, host a website reveal party to celebrate your digital accomplishment.

Think about how you access information in today's world. You probably "Google it" right? Given this assumption, it's in an educator's best interest to begin understanding the role digital content plays at a learning, teaching, and branding level. Leveraging the power of digital tools, such as Google Sites, is now a major responsibility for educational institutions.

HACK 29

MOVE THE CONVERSATION FORWARD WITH BLOGGER

THE PROBLEM: WHO IS TELLING YOUR SCHOOL STORY?

IF YOU DO not tell your own classroom, school, or district story, somebody else will, and they'll tell it from their own perspective, not yours. Social media networks, including blogs, have supported stakeholders' efforts to get the word out about certain topics. A tweet, Facebook post, or blog post can be extremely positive or incredibly negative. Teachers, principals, and superintendents sometimes overlook the power of branding all the awesome things that are taking place. Too often they allow others to control the narrative in the physical and virtual worlds. Think about it for a second. Don't you notice all of the negative publicity out there about schools and educators? Any time something goes slightly wrong, it's front page news. A reader has to dig deep into a newspaper or website to find positive articles related to a school initiative or student achievement.

Digital reputation is just as important as any other. Building a rock-solid reputation does not happen overnight. If you take it one day at a time and slowly build up your online reputation, things will begin to look up. Connecting with stakeholders in the virtual world through a tool like a blog can be very engaging. Students can use a blog to show what they know about a topic and

> Users can add text, images, videos, hyperlinks, and so much more to tell and publish their stories for the world to enjoy.

gain perspective from others in another part of the world. Teachers can highlight classroom happenings to parents through a weekly blast. Districts can inform stakeholders about district-wide events, budgetary items, and initiatives. When you change the narrative, you change the culture.

THE HACK: SHARE YOUR STORY WITH BLOGGER

Change the educational conversation with Blogger. If you are looking for a chance to connect with others and share a story, Blogger is the tool for you. It's Google's answer to a blogging platform. You can share insight through a few sentences or several paragraphs. Users can add text, images, videos, hyperlinks, and so much more to tell and publish their stories for the world to enjoy.

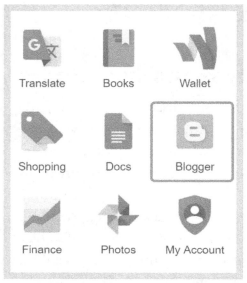

Image 29.1 Google and the Google logo are registered trademarks lof Google Inc., used with permission.

To make this happen, click the waffle from the Gmail screen and locate the "Blogger" icon to gain access. Take a look at Image 29.1 to see what the Blogger icon looks like. Once inside Blogger you will see the main page and in the middle an orange button titled "Create New Blog." Click this button and give your blog a title. For this example, we will call our blog "Hacking Google for Education." For the address we simplified things and used hackgoogleedu.blogspot.com. You will notice that in Blogger the subdomain defaults to blogspot.com. This can be changed later to a domain you already own. Next you will want to pick a template, which can be changed later if needed.

Once inside Blogger, you will need to skim through the various features it has to offer. On the left-hand side you will notice such tabs as Posts, Stats, Pages, Layout, Template, and Settings. Each time you visit Blogger you will automatically start in the Posts area. Let's create your very first Blogger blog post: Click the orange button titled "New Post." The next page is where you will compose your first blog post. Give your post a catchy title. Don't worry, you can change the title at any time.

As you skim through the editing features, you will notice they look very similar to most other word processing programs. Feel free to add images or hyperlinks. You will notice a "Save" button in the upper right-hand corner of the screen. You can click this as many times as you want, but the blog post will save automatically just like any other Google product. Want to see what your blog post will look like once it's published? Click the "Preview" button that is located next to the "Save" button.

The Post Settings allow your blog post to be found online and determine the way in which you want readers to interact with the content. The first tab under Post Settings is titled "Labels." This is where you will want to provide keywords for your blog post so it can be found during a search. For example, you could use such labels as technology or education. The next tab is titled "Schedule" and gives you the option of automatically pushing out your blog post once the publish button is clicked or selecting a date and time for your blog post to go live. The "Permalink" tab will show you the URL for this particular blog post. Feel free to create a custom permalink if the mood strikes you.

The "Location" tab can link your blog post to a geographic location. In Settings, you can choose from a number of options, the most important being a reader's ability to comment on your blog post. Some bloggers like feedback from readers and others do not. Once you feel that your blog post is ready for the world to see, go ahead and click the orange "Publish" button at the top of the page.

What YOU Can Do Tomorrow

CLASSROOM: Get students blogging to bring attention to an important issue. Blogging turns a static writing assignment into an interactive experience. Let your students experience what it's like to share their insight on a topic with their peers and possibly with other students from a different part of the world. Before students actually start blogging, it's important to provide them with some background knowledge on how the process works.

You might have students write a practice blog post on a piece of paper and then ask their classmates to post sticky notes as a way of commenting. This lets them into the world of blogging without actually publishing content in the digital world. The next step would be to go over how to use Blogger. For their first attempt at blogging, allow your students to share the blogs with other students in the same class or building. Once they're used to the dynamic you can find other schools from around the world to share your students' blog posts.

SCHOOL: Publish a monthly report on your school's blog, highlighting student and staff achievements. One of Brad's responsibilities as a building leader is to curate a monthly report that gets pushed out to stakeholders virtually. He will create and disseminate a Google Form to collect content from staff. For example, staff will provide information about projects students are working on or initiatives that their clubs are involved with. Once the information is collected, Brad organizes the information in the form of a blog post and pushes it out to stakeholders via email, social media feeds, and the school website.

DISTRICT: Maintain a video blog or vlog that houses stakeholder-created video clips associated with the various schools in your district. A forward-thinking goal for any superintendent would be to capture the unbelievable things going on throughout the district to share with the public. Each week, stakeholders could submit video clips of educational experiences. These clips could then be uploaded and embedded to the district blog. The blog itself could be located on your district website and pushed out through your alert system, social media channels, and applications.

Blogger is a great way to promote your district and keep the focus on the positive. Providing a consistent message to your stakeholders establishes trust and a sense of pride. Commit to blogging and supporting the blogging efforts of stakeholders. Remember that classrooms, schools, and districts need to control the narrative, both in virtual and physical worlds. Don't assume that stakeholders know about what is taking place. What are you waiting for? Start getting the word out right now!

HACK 30

TRANSLATE DOCUMENTS FOR STAKEHOLDERS

THE PROBLEM: IMPORTANT EDUCATION-RELATED DOCUMENTS ARE NOT IN A STAKEHOLDER'S NATIVE LANGUAGE

PLACE YOURSELF IN the shoes of another person who does not speak your language. Better yet, pretend that you are a student who just moved to another country. You have no idea how to speak, read, or write the native language. Not only do you have to acclimate yourself to the culture of the school and society, but you have to quickly learn the language that your classmates are accustomed to using. It might take months, or more realistically, years to learn a whole new language and way of life.

> **Schools need to meet families where they are, and that includes communicating effectively by way of translation services.**

Luckily, technology has evolved so much over the years that people are now able to upload, type, or speak into an online program and have a translation conducted in seconds. Google Translate does just this, making a student's or parent's transition into a new country a bit more bearable.

THE HACK: USE THE GOOGLE TRANSLATE FEATURE TO ASSIST STAKEHOLDERS WHO SPEAK ANOTHER LANGUAGE

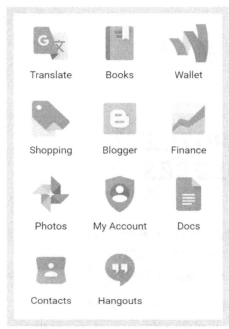

Image 30.1 Google and the Google logo are registered trademarks of Google Inc., used with permission.

Access Google Translate using the waffle in the upper right corner of your Gmail screen or by conducting a Google search. Image 30.1 shows an example of what the app looks like. Scan the screen to see what this program has to offer. You will notice that there are two boxes. The box on the left provides users with a place to type, speak, and hear the word they want translated. The translated word appears in the box on the right.

Some other helpful features contained in these boxes allow users to use a virtual keyboard, save or share translated words, and offer edits. Users can also flip flop the words being translated by clicking the double arrow icon in the middle. There are over seventy-five languages to choose from including English, French, Spanish, Arabic, Korean, and Ukrainian. You can translate up to 5,000 characters at a time or upload a document.

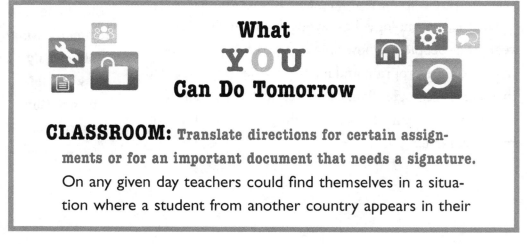

What YOU Can Do Tomorrow

CLASSROOM: Translate directions for certain assignments or for an important document that needs a signature. On any given day teachers could find themselves in a situation where a student from another country appears in their class. Sometimes these students do not speak the language that is prevalent in the classroom. In most cases these students should be supported with some sort of ELL program. A helpful practice in addition to these supports would be to use Google Translate to translate directions for assignments and send home translated documents to be reviewed by parents.

SCHOOL: Translate school-related documents such as field trip forms and athletic participation forms. Schools must be mindful of their populations, particularly when it comes to language barriers. Every single family must be able to read important documents. Many schools are digitizing their forms and requiring parents to fill them out online. Google Translate could help schools translate these important documents and make them available online.

DISTRICT: Translate district information and documents that need to be made available to all stakeholders. Kindergarten registration, vaccine documentation, and graduation documents are just a few of the many items that can be translated into another language for families that reside in your district. Simply copy and paste or upload the documents to Google Translate. Then you can take the translated information and disseminate it on paper or online.

A school or district committed to promoting the success of all students must translate important information and documents for stakeholders. Google Translate simplifies this process to ensure that everyone is on the same page. It's imperative that you work alongside your ELL staff and conduct an audit of sorts to determine what actually needs to be translated. Making this information and documentation available on paper and digitally is crucial. Schools need to meet families where they are, and that includes communicating effectively by way of translation services. As you embark on this essential method of connecting with all your stakeholders, be sure to confirm the accuracy of your translated message. From time to time the translation does not accurately depict the message you wish to send. It is always best to confirm accuracy before sending to families.

HACK 31

MOBILIZE WITH GOOGLE PLAY

THE PROBLEM: STAYING CONNECTED
WHEN YOU'RE NOT AT YOUR DESKTOP

BUSY EDUCATORS ARE not always able to look at a desktop during the day. Google has developed a store called Google Play that is supported on all Android phones. This allows educators to get the best out of Google from their mobile devices. Educators on the go need to be able to check in on their phones. You can even use your mobile device in the classroom. Billy and his co-teacher use ClassDojo with their students to build a positive classroom environment. The ClassDojo app that is available on Billy's Android device allows for him to walk around and update his students' progress so he does not have to be tied down to a computer.

> **Play Store allows mobile users to stay connected to their Google accounts no matter where they are.**

THE HACK: ANDROID DEVICES ALLOW
YOU TO BE MOBILE IN SCHOOL

Educators who own an Android device can open up their Play Store and search for all the apps that they have on their desktop. You can download almost all of the G Suite Programs, including Google Drive, Docs, Sheets, Slides, Classroom, Maps, and Keep. In a collaborative setting, you can even have more than one person adding to the G Suite products to enhance the experience for everyone. One person can be working on a desktop version while another person can be working on a mobile phone.

What
YOU
Can Do Tomorrow

CLASSROOM: Google Keep helps you stay on track with checklists. Educators no longer need to be tied down to a desk. You can take your cellphone with you and check in with students and check their work using Google Keep. You can show students where they should be in their progress on an assignment and make sure they are on task. If your school has a bring-your-own-device policy, you can even allow students to use Keep on their phones to check their progress. See the app on Scott's phone in Image 31.1— look on the bottom right just above the unwieldy number of emails he has from Brad and Billy in his inbox. Clearly he needs to reread Hack 3 and get it back under control. Check out Hack 13 for details on how to use Google Keep.

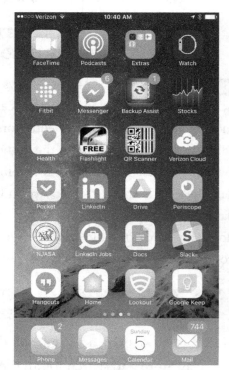

Image 31.1 Google and the Google logo are registered trademarks of Google Inc., used with permission.

SCHOOL: Sync Google Photos with ease. Take Google Photos with your Android phone and sync them to your Google account for easy access. When you are walking around a school building, snap pictures of the great things that are going on and have it sync to your Google Photos. When you get back to your computer, you can use those pictures for a newsletter or tweet the photos out.

DISTRICT: Nudge your colleagues' memories with Remind.

One of the best apps that you can download is Remind. This intuitive app allows people to get text alerts about important events or announcements. Parents can subscribe to different groups for alerts and decide which alerts they want to be notified of. The district can have one group for important announcements, such as school closings.

Play Store allows mobile users to stay connected to their Google accounts no matter where they are. There are many third-party apps, like Remind, that enhance the users' experience of Google.

HACK 32

GO GOOGLE WITH APPLE

THE PROBLEM: APPLE DEVICE USERS
WANT ACCESS TO GOOGLE APPS

YOU MIGHT BE an Apple junkie who is addicted to such devices as the iPhone, iPad, and MacBook Air. You might be wondering how to use Google apps on your Apple devices. In fact, at this very moment you may not even be contemplating making the shift to Google, thinking that it just will not be worth your time. Several years ago this sort of thing would be an issue, but no longer. Developers at Google have developed apps that can be downloaded onto your Apple devices.

Apple makes these apps available for iPhones and iPads in the App Store. This flexibility helps schools where students and staff bring in their own devices. Some districts are 1:1 with iPads and also use the G Suite for Education platform. Students and staff can now take full advantage of their school-issued Google accounts on their Apple devices.

> You can start working on your iPhone and pick up where you left off later on another device.

THE HACK: GOOGLE CAN BE USED ON APPLE

Download some of the more than fifty Google Incorporated apps that currently reside in the App Store on your iPhone or iPad. Locate the blue App Store icon on your device and search the word Google. Browse through the many Google apps that are available. Some that you might find interesting or useful are Google Photos, Google Translate, Google Street View, and Google Arts and Culture. Make sure it's made by Google Inc. Once you have selected an app, tap the download button. When you activate the app for the first time it will ask you to link it with your Google account. Don't worry—most of the Google apps for the iPhone and iPad allow users to flip back and forth between multiple Google accounts. You can start working on your iPhone and pick up where you left off later on another device.

What
YOU
Can Do Tomorrow

CLASSROOM: Download the Google Classroom app onto your iPhone. Teachers can continue to communicate, assign, assess, and collaborate on a mobile device as long as they are in a G Suite for Education district. Refer to the Google Classroom chapter for application ideas. Teachers and students can now access their virtual classrooms on their mobile devices. The Google Classroom iPhone app allows you to do some unique things that are not yet available on the desktop version, like snap and upload a picture and mark up an assignment that contains a PDF, Google Doc, or Google Slide. While on an iPhone at home or in school, students will open the Google Classroom app, tap the assignment, and then tap the file. A pen and disk icon appears on top of the screen. These modify and ultimately save the documents. The same sort of workflow you would expect to experience on a laptop or desktop is now available on an iPhone or iPad.

SCHOOL: Push out a Google Slide presentation from your iPhone to a nearby Apple TV mirroring device with the Google Slide app. You can use your iPhone as a clicker. Students or staff may bring their phones to school and use their devices to support their Google Slide presentations. Some schools have Apple TVs installed in their classrooms so students and teachers can share work with the rest of the class by tapping the screen a few times. If you don't have Apple TV take a look at Hack 18 for similar ideas.

If you find yourself in a pinch and need to update a Google Slide presentation for an upcoming staff meeting but do not have access to a laptop, you can hop onto the Google Slide app and make the necessary updates. Remember that Google apps reside in the cloud, so you can open and update from any device and pick up later where you left off without ever having to click the "save" button.

DISTRICT: Translate text, images, and other types of information with the Google Translate app to help support stakeholders during meetings, visitations, and events. Once it's downloaded to your device, browse through the amazing features of the app. Users can speak, write, and type and have their words translated from one language to another. This app could be beneficial for both school officials and visitors. During Back to School Night or Open House, educational content and important messages could be translated to assist with comprehension. This app also provides a great opportunity for stakeholders to gain perspective and learn about the languages of different cultures that make up their district community.

Google apps on the iPhone and iPad are accessible on almost all internet-enabled devices, can serve many purposes, and maximize time. Learning, teaching, and leading can take place anywhere and at any time. Parents and students now have access to a vast support network that extends beyond the classroom walls.

HACK 33

AMP UP YOUR GOOGLE PRODUCTIVITY WITH THESE QUICK FIXES

THE PROBLEM: I NEED TO BECOME MORE PRODUCTIVE WITH GOOGLE

USING THE GOOGLE Suite for Education provides educators with numerous options to share and collaborate. We have also learned how to make things work more easily for us, which makes us more productive. In the first 32 chapters we fit hacks into categories that you can easily follow, but sometimes we find hacks that don't fit so easily into a category even though they are worth sharing because they will make you more productive. These are quick and easy hacks that will help you as an educator, and they can be used at the classroom, school, and/or district level.

THE HACK: FIND A HACK AND BECOME A MORE PRODUCTIVE EDUCATOR

Whether you use Google at the classroom, school, or district level, you probably want to become more productive. In this last chapter we share some favorite techniques we have used over the years that have made us

> We use technology to become more productive and efficient in our responsibilities as educators.

more productive in our roles as a classroom teacher, vice principal, and superintendent. They get our hack seal of approval. Look through the list, find a strategy, and give it a try.

What
YOU
Can Do Tomorrow

CLASSROOM: Create a more productive classroom for you and your students with these simple hacks.

Change font to uppercase

Download the "Change Case" Google Docs Add-on to a new or existing document. You can change letters to uppercase, lowercase, or capitalize initial letters. Don't retype it; use the app.

Cite a source

Citing resources when writing a paper can be tedious. Scott often talks about the frustration of individually looking up formatting rules and then typing his reference list for his dissertation before a good app was available. That frustration no longer needs to exist. Open up a Google Doc and click the "Explore" icon in the lower right-hand corner of the screen. You will notice that a dialogue box appears on the right with three options to choose from: Web, Images, and Drive. Go to the Web option and type in a word that you want to research. Hover to the right of the result you want to use and a quote icon will appear. Click on the quote icon and you will notice that the citation has been inserted into your Google Doc. You can change the format of your citation by clicking the three dots and selecting MLA, APA, or Chicago.

SCHOOL: Develop a more productive school environment when running meetings or events for faculty or parents.

Force others to make a copy of your file

You probably share files with staff and parents from your

drive, but you may not want people to edit the original. Forcing others to make a copy of your file allows people to make their own copies of a Google Document, Google Slide, Google Drawing, Google Form, or Google Sheet without editing your original.

Simply open the document that you want someone else to copy, locate the web address on the top of the screen, and change the word from "edit" to "copy." Then you can share or embed the new web address that ends with the word "copy" to others. You can also share a link with others and force them to make a copy by changing the word at the end of the link from "edit" to "copy." See Image 33.1 to see how to change the link and send the new link. The recipient will be prompted to make a copy when they click the link.

https://docs.google.com/document/d/1H1g81TSpxT9O8NgDnR6WehReFqrCT7PQo2rAoNqXAYl/edit?usp=sharing

https://docs.google.com/document/d/1H1g81TSpxT9O8NgDnR6WehReFqrCT7PQo2rAoNqXAYl/copy

Image 33.1 Google and the Google logo are registered trademarks of Google Inc., used with permission.

Timer and stopwatch

If you need to set a time limit, see how long it takes you to do something, or establish a time for a team-building activity, search the word "timer" and a timer/stopwatch will appear at the top of your search screen. You can select "timer" or "stopwatch" depending on your needs. Click on the time to modify the amount of time you need for the task at hand. An alert will go off when the timer runs out. You can also go into full-screen mode for both the time and stopwatch.

DISTRICT: Gather information from stakeholders during a presentation or provide information to them with a shorter URL. District presentations can be more engaging if you embed opportunities for those watching to be involved. You also want to provide participants opportunities to access information without having to type in long and often hard to read URLs. Here are a few that work.

Embed a Poll Everywhere poll into a Slide presentation

Real-time feedback enriches a presentation. Download the "Poll Everywhere" Google Slide extension from the Chrome Store. Then, open up a new Google Slide presentation and you notice that a new tab called Poll Everywhere appears at the top of the screen. You can create a new poll or insert a previously created poll. Once in presentation mode it will appear in your presentation for audience members to access.

Google URL Shortener

Sometimes you want to share a link with someone during a presentation or meeting. More often than not, the link is too long to jot down or it's copied incorrectly. Use Google URL Shortener to shrink the web address that you want to share with another person. To access, conduct a Google search for "Google URL Shortener" or type in this web address https://goo.gl, then copy and paste the link you want to truncate into the shortener. You will notice that a shortened version of the original URL is now available to be copied and pasted, shared with other people, or projected on a screen. When people type the shortened URL into their browser, they will arrive at the website.

We use technology to become more productive and efficient in our responsibilities as educators. We hope that using it will give us more time to teach in the classroom, create a more effective learning environment in the school, and provide more opportunities for the community to engage at the district level. Although these quick-fix hacks don't fit in one of our other 32 categories they do make us more productive in our roles.

CONCLUSION

HACKING GOOGLE FOR Education is a robust guide to edtech that can be implemented at the classroom, school, and district levels. Its main objective is to move educators from good to great and promote the success of all students. The hacks throughout the book provide teachers, principals, and superintendents with a wide array of digital strategies to innovate learning spaces and drive change.

After reading this book you might be overwhelmed, thinking that every hack needs to implemented immediately. This assumption is far from true. If you only research one hack and use it to enhance your impact as an educator, then that is perfectly fine. Our focus is to get you to take a risk and try something new to make your environment either more efficient or more collaborative in nature.

For any of the hacks to truly work, people need time and support. If you are a building- or district-level administrator and a colleague comes to you excited about using a particular hack from the book, support them. Give them time during the school day to dig deep into how the hack can impact teaching and learning. Help them, and support their efforts during the implementation phase, even if things go wrong at first.

Truly committing to the Google way of life in an educational setting takes months and years, not hours and days. Those who are now confident in their ability to learn, teach, or lead in a G Suite for Education environment feel this way because they were able to problem-solve obstacles and move full steam ahead.

Just as with any other successful implementation, initiative, or program, a balanced approach ensures that all stakeholders' needs are met. A solid understanding of how to connect with students, an ability to integrate pedagogically sound teaching methods, a passion for making subjects relevant, and a commitment to lead with a collaborative mindset will sync well with the G Suite for Education environment. The ideas you glean from this book will provide you with additional "tools of the trade" that will help you help kids.

What sort of hacks are up your sleeve? We would love to know, and so would the rest of the world. Hop onto your favorite social networking site like Twitter and share your knowledge through our #HackGoogleEdu hashtag. Use it to join us as we discuss the hacks in this book and share your own hacks so we keep the learning and sharing moving forward. Our online community is only as good as your next tweet, so please share often. If Twitter is not your thing, consider joining the Hacking Google for Education Google+ Community. Either way, you will be able to continue the conversation from this book and help others move in a positive direction.

Good luck and hack away!

OTHER BOOKS IN THE
HACK LEARNING SERIES

HACKING EDUCATION
10 Quick Fixes For Every School

By Mark Barnes (@markbarnes19) & Jennifer Gonzalez (@cultofpedagogy)

In the bestselling *Hacking Education*, Mark Barnes and Jennifer Gonzalez employ decades of teaching experience and hundreds of discussions with education thought leaders to show you how to find and hone the quick fixes that every school and classroom need. Using a Hacker's mentality, they provide **one Aha moment after another** with 10 Quick Fixes For Every School—solutions to everyday problems and teaching methods that any teacher or administrator can implement immediately.

"Barnes and Gonzalez don't just solve problems; they turn teachers into hackers—a transformation that is right on time."

— **DON WETTRICK**, AUTHOR OF *PURE GENIUS*

Make Writing
5 Teaching Strategies That Turn Writer's
Workshop Into a Maker Space

By Angela Stockman (@angelastockman)

Everyone's favorite education blogger and writing coach, Angela Stockman, turns teaching strategies and practices upside down in the bestselling, *Make Writing*. She spills you out of your chair, shreds your lined paper, and launches you and your writer's workshop into the maker space! Stockman provides five right-now writing strategies that reinvent instruction and **inspire both young and adult writers** to express ideas with tools that have rarely, if ever, been considered. *Make Writing* is a fast-paced journey inside Stockman's Western New York Young Writer's Studio, alongside the students there who learn how to write and how to make, employing Stockman's unique teaching methods.

"Offering suggestions for using new materials in old ways, thoughtful questions, and specific tips for tinkering and finding new audiences, this refreshing book is inspiring and practical in equal measure."

— **AMY LUDWIG VANDERWATER**, AUTHOR AND TEACHER

HACKING ASSESSMENT
10 Ways to Go Gradeless in a Traditional Grades School

By Starr Sackstein (@mssackstein)

In the bestselling *Hacking Assessment,* award-winning teacher and world-renowned formative assessment expert Starr Sackstein unravels one of education's oldest mysteries: How to assess learning without grades—even in a school that uses numbers, letters, GPAs, and report cards. While many educators can only muse about the possibility of a world without grades, teachers like Sackstein are **reimagining education**. In this unique, eagerly anticipated book, Sackstein shows you exactly how to create a remarkable no-grades classroom like hers, a vibrant place where students grow, share, thrive, and become independent learners who never ask, "What's this worth?"

"The beauty of the book is that it is not an empty argument against grades—but rather filled with valuable alternatives that are practical and will help to refocus the classroom on what matters most."

— **ADAM BELLOW**, WHITE HOUSE PRESIDENTIAL INNOVATION FELLOW

HACKING THE COMMON CORE
10 Strategies for Amazing Learning in a Standardized World

By Michael Fisher (@fisher1000)

In *Hacking the Common Core,* longtime teacher and CCSS specialist Mike Fisher shows you how to bring fun back to learning, with 10 amazing hacks for teaching all Core subjects, while engaging students and making learning fun. Fisher's experience and insights help teachers and parents better understand close reading, balancing fiction and non-fiction, using projects with the Core and much more. *Hacking the Common Core* provides **read-tonight-implement-tomorrow strategies** for teaching the standards in fun and engaging ways, improving teaching and learning for students, parents, and educators.

HACKING LEADERSHIP
10 Ways Great Leaders Inspire Learning That Teachers, Students, and Parents Love

By Joe Sanfelippo (@joesanfelippoFC) and Tony Sinanis (@tonysinanis)

In the runaway bestseller *Hacking Leadership*, renowned school leaders Joe Sanfelippo and Tony Sinanis bring readers inside schools that few stakeholders have ever seen—places where students not only come first but have a unique voice in teaching and learning. Sanfelippo and Sinanis ignore the bureaucracy that stifles many leaders, focusing instead on building a culture of **engagement, transparency, and most important, fun.** *Hacking Leadership* has superintendents, principals, and teacher leaders around the world employing strategies they never before believed possible.

"The authors do a beautiful job of helping leaders focus inward, instead of outward. This is an essential read for leaders who are, or want to lead, learner-centered schools."
— GEORGE COUROS, AUTHOR OF *THE INNOVATOR'S MINDSET*

HACKING LITERACY
5 Ways To Turn Any Classroom Into a Culture Of Readers

By Gerard Dawson (@gerarddawson3)

In *Hacking Literacy*, classroom teacher, author, and reading consultant Gerard Dawson reveals 5 simple ways any educator or parent can turn even the most reluctant reader into a thriving, enthusiastic lover of books. Dawson cuts through outdated pedagogy and standardization, turning reading theory into practice, sharing **valuable reading strategies,** and providing what *Hack Learning Series* readers have come to expect—actionable, do-it-tomorrow strategies that can be built into long-term solutions.

HACKING ENGAGEMENT
50 Tips & Tools to Engage Teachers and Learners Daily

By James Alan Sturtevant (@jamessturtevant)

Some students hate your class. Others are just bored. Many are too nice, or too afraid, to say anything about it. Don't let it bother you; it happens to the best of us. But now, it's **time to engage!** In

Hacking Engagement, the seventh book in the *Hack Learning Series*, veteran high school teacher, author, and popular podcaster James Sturtevant provides 50—that's right five-oh—tips and tools that will engage even the most reluctant learners daily.

HACKING HOMEWORK
10 Strategies That Inspire Learning Outside the Classroom

By Starr Sackstein (@mssackstein) and Connie Hamilton (@conniehamilton)

Learning outside the classroom is being reimagined, and student engagement is better than ever. World-renowned author/educator Starr Sackstein has changed how teachers around the world look at traditional grades. Now she's teaming with veteran educator, curriculum director, and national presenter Connie Hamilton to bring you **10 powerful strategies** for teachers and parents that promise to inspire independent learning at home, without punishments or low grades.

"Starr Sackstein and Connie Hamilton have assembled a book full of great answers to the question, 'How can we make homework engaging and meaningful?'"
— **DOUG FISHER & NANCY FREY**, AUTHORS/PRESENTERS

HACKING PROJECT BASED LEARNING
10 Easy Steps to PBL and Inquiry in the Classroom

By Ross Cooper (@rosscoops31) and Erin Murphy (@murphysmusings5)

As questions and mysteries around PBL and inquiry continue to swirl, experienced classroom teachers and school administrators Ross Cooper and Erin Murphy have written a book that will empower those intimidated by PBL to cry, "I can do this!" while at the same time providing added value for those who are already familiar with the process. *Hacking Project Based Learning* demystifies what PBL is all about with **10 hacks that construct a simple path** that educators and students can easily follow to achieve success.

"*Hacking Project Based Learning* is a classroom essential. Its ten simple 'hacks' will guide you through the process of setting up a learning environment in which students will thrive from start to finish."
— **DANIEL H. PINK**, *NEW YORK TIMES* BESTSELLING AUTHOR OF *DRIVE*

HACK LEARNING ANTHOLOGY
Innovative Solutions for Teachers and Leaders

Edited by Mark Barnes (@markbarnes19)

Anthology brings you the most innovative education Hacks from the first nine books in the *Hack Learning Series*. Written by 12 award-winning classroom teachers, principals, superintendents, college instructors, and international presenters, *Anthology* is every educator's new problem-solving handbook. It is both a preview of 9 other books and a **full-fledged, feature-length blueprint** for solving your biggest school and classroom problems.

HACK LEARNING RESOURCES

All Things Hack Learning:

hacklearning.org

The Entire Hack Learning Series on Amazon:

hacklearningbooks.com

The Hack Learning Podcast, hosted by Mark Barnes:

hacklearningpodcast.com

The Hacking Engagement Podcast, hosted by James Sturtevant:

jamesalansturtevant.com

Hack Learning on Twitter:

@HackMyLearning

#HackLearning

#HackingLeadership

#HackingLiteracy

#HackingEngagement

#HackingHomework

#HackingPBL

#MakeWriting

#HackGoogleEdu

Hack Learning on Facebook:

facebook.com/hacklearningseries

Hack Learning on Instagram:

hackmylearning

The Hack Learning Academy:

hacklearningacademy.com

MEET THE AUTHORS

Brad Currie is the Supervisor of Instruction and Assistant Principal for the Chester School District in Chester, New Jersey, where he has led a 1:1 Chromebook program for the past four years. He is the 2017 NJPSA Visionary Assistant Principal of the Year, 2017 NASSP National Assistant Principal of the Year, and a 2014 ASCD Emerging Leader. Brad is a Founding Partner for Evolving Educators LLC and the co-founder of #Satchat, an online Twitter discussion for current and emerging school leaders. He is a Google Certified Trainer, author, blogger, presenter, and adjunct professor. Learn more about Brad by following him on Twitter @bradmcurrie or visiting www.evolvingeducators.com.

Billy Krakower is the Computer Technology Instructor, Gifted & Talented, STEAM Teacher for grades three and four. He is also a co-teacher of ELA for Special Education students at Beatrice Gilmore Elementary School in the Woodland Park Public School District. He is a 2014 ASCD Emerging Leader. Billy is a Founding Partner for Evolving Educators LLC and the co-moderator of #Satchat, an online Twitter discussion for current and emerging school leaders. He is a Microsoft Certified Educator, author, blogger and presenter. Learn more about Billy by following him on Twitter @wkrakower or visiting www.evolvingeducators.com.

Scott Rocco, Ed.D. is a superintendent in New Jersey, adjunct professor, instructor in the NJEXCEL program, co-founder/co-moderator of #Satchat, founder of #ASuperDay on Twitter, an EdCampNJ organizer, conference presenter, and keynote speaker. Before becoming a superintendent, Scott was an assistant superintendent, elementary principal, middle school vice principal, and a high school and middle school social studies teacher. In his first stint as superintendent, Scott spearheaded the initiative to "Go Google" as a district. This successful transition to G Suite for Education sparked more collaboration among students, teachers, and all stakeholders. Scott presents at conferences on the use of social media for educators, school safety, marketing yourself, and various leadership topics. He has delivered keynote addresses across the United States and is dedicated to positively and productively engaging educators in a dialogue that improves student learning, enhances instruction, and creates effective learning environments for all who attend and work in schools. Learn more about Scott by following him on Twitter @ScottRRocco or visiting www.evolvingeducators.com.

ACKNOWLEDGEMENTS

Brad

I dedicate this book to my amazing wife, Leigh, who is an unbelievable educator and parent. To my son, Cooper, a hard-working fifth-grader who can't wait to get a signed copy of this book. And to my daughter, Sydney, a feisty kindergartner who loves to draw inside expensive books. I would also like to dedicate this book to the amazing educators I work with on a continuous basis in the Chester School District.

Billy

I dedicate this book to my amazing wife, Jennifer, who has put up with me while taking on another book project. To my daughter, Brianna, who would often be pulling at my leg or wanting to sit on my lap and play with me as I was working on this book.

Scott

I dedicate this book to my awesome wife, Tracy, who always takes care of our family while I'm working on something. I'd also like to dedicate this book to my three children: Paige, Nicholas, and Michael, who often ground me in the idea that I might be a little too nerdy! Thanks #Squad.

All

All three of us would like to personally thank our amazing PLN who are all so supportive. Their dedication to #Satchat and our other projects is always appreciated and never taken for granted.

Finally, a special thank you to our colleagues and friends, Chrissy Romano-Arribito and Adam Schoenbart, who each made small, yet powerful, contributions to this book.

PUBLICATIONS

Times 10 is helping all education stakeholders improve every aspect of teaching and learning. We are committed to solving big problems with simple ideas. We bring you content from experts, shared through multiple channels, including books, podcasts, and an array of social networks. Our mantra is simple: Read it today; fix it tomorrow.

Stay in touch with us at #HackLearning on Twitter and on the Hack Learning Facebook page. To work with our authors and consultants, visit our Team page at hacklearning.org.